Marketing Decisions Made Accurate and Easy

Understanding and Using Marketing Power Tools ...Everyone Can Use – For Life!

James W. Stark

Baker Colleges of Michigan

McGraw-Hill Primis
Custom Publishing

New York St. Louis San Francisco Auckland Bogotá
Caracas Lisbon London Madrid Mexico Milan Montreal
New Delhi Paris San Juan Singapore Sydney Tokyo Toronto

McGraw-Hill Higher Education
A Division of The McGraw-Hill Companies

Marketing Decisions Made Accurate and Easy
Understanding and Using Marketing Power Tools
...Everyone Can Use – For Life!

McGraw-Hill's Primis Custom Publishing Series consists of products that are produced from camera-ready copy. Peer review, class testing, and accuracy are primarily the responsibility of the author(s).

14 15 16 17 18 19 20 QSR QSR 0 9 8 7

ISBN-13: 978-0-07-253222-7
ISBN-10: 0-07-253222-X

Editor: Tom Lyons
Cover Design: Maggie Lytle
Printer/Binder: Quebecor World

Table of Contents

Baker College Campus Locations

AUBURN HILLS
1500 University Drive
Auburn Hills, MI 48326
PH: (248) 340-0600
or 1-888-429-0410
FAX: (248) 340-0608

BRIGHTON
Brighton High School
7878 Brighton Road
Brighton, MI 48116
PH: (810) BAKER-00 (225-3700)
or 1-800-964-4299
FAX: (810) 766-4255

CADILLAC
9600 East 13th Street
Cadillac, MI 49601
PH: (231) 876-3100
or 1-888-313-3463
FAX: (231) 775-8505

CASS CITY
6667 Main Street
Cass City, MI 48726
PH: (517) 872-1129
or 1-800-964-4299
FAX: (517) 872-1130

FLINT
1050 West Bristol Road
Flint, MI 48507
PH: (810) 766-4000
or 1-800-964-4299
FAX: (810) 766-4255

FREMONT
c/o Newaygo County
Educational Service Center
4747 W. 48th Street
Fremont, MI 49412
PH: (231) 924-8850
or 1-800-937-0337
FAX: (231) 924-8808

JACKSON
2800 Springport Road
Jackson, MI 49202
PH: (517) 788-7800
or 1-888-343-3683
FAX: (517) 789-7331

CLINTON TOWNSHIP
34950 Little Mack Avenue
Clinton Township, MI 48035
PH: (810) 791-6610
or 1-888-272-2842
FAX: (810) 791-6611

MUSKEGON
1903 Marquette Avenue
Muskegon, MI 49442
PH: (231) 777-5200
or 1-800-937-0337
FAX: (231) 777-5201

OWOSSO
1020 S. Washington Street
Owosso, MI 48867
PH: (517) 729-3350
or 1-800-879-3797
FAX: (517) 729-3359

PORT HURON
3403 Lapeer Road
Port Huron, MI 48060
PH: (810) 985-7000
or 1-888-262-2442
FAX: (810) 985-7066

SANDUSKY
Sanilac County Health
Department Building
171 Dawson
Sandusky, MI 48471
PH: 1-888-262-2442

WEST BRANCH
National City Bank – Downtown
113 Houghton Ave.
West Branch, MI 48661
PH: (517) 345-2995
or 1-800-964-4299
FAX: (810) 766-4255

WILLIAMSTON
c/o Williamston Area
Community Center
201 School Street
Williamston, MI 48895
PH: (517) 655-6216
or 1-800-879-3797
FAX: (517) 723-3359

**BUSINESS & CORPORATE
SERVICES**
1050 West Bristol Road
Flint, MI 48507
PH: (810) 766-4242
FAX: (810) 232-7540

**CENTER FOR
GRADUATE STUDIES**
1050 West Bristol Road
Flint, MI 48507
PH: (810) 766-4390
or 1-800-469-3165
FAX: (810) 766-4399

**BAKER COLLEGE
ON-LINE**
1050 West Bristol Road
Flint, MI 48507
PH: (810) 766-4390
or 1-800-469-4062
FAX: (810) 766-4399
online.baker.edu

Moving Marketing From the Abstract to Process Thinking, Problem Solving, Decision-Making

Introduction:

When a carpenter puts on his tool belt, there is a place in the belt for each tool of the trade. I sometimes walk into my first Principles of Marketing class wearing a carpenter's tool belt. Without saying a word, I place two pieces of board on the desk. Then, pretending to need, measure, and make a cut in one of the boards, I estimate the length of the cut using my fingers. Making a mark on the board by using a small saw, I then put the saw down and make a cut using the claw end of the hammer virtually beating the board into submission. Next I proceed to nail the two obviously unrelated boards together, driving the nails with the casing on my tape ruler. Then I say, ***"Boy, I sure hope this works!"***

This is the first time I look up at the members of the class. I simply say, *"What is wrong with this picture?"* Without hesitation, most students will offer an assessment of what I did that not only looked ignorant, but was very inefficient. This is when I drop the bomb. *"Then why do so many marketing people try to market without using the tools of the trade, use so inefficiently the ones they have in their tool belt, and end up thinking, **"Boy, I sure hope this works?"***

This is the primary purpose of this book. The tools of the marketing profession are similar, in function, to a carpenter's task for: assessing the needs of the job, bringing in the correct material, assembling a product using the proper tools, and being very efficient in the process making the end result something desired by the consumer. In marketing terms we say, situation analysis, opportunity, strategies and confidence level.

Within the context of marketing are four primary areas of concern that, when put together into a package, are referred to as the market mix. This mix is made up of the product or service being marketed, the advertising or promoting of the product to consumers, the availability of the product through a distribution system sometimes referred to as placement, and the pricing strategy used in selling the product to consumers. These are the 4 Ps of marketing; i.e. product, price, placement, and promotion.

We are going to address many marketing tools, learn how each tool works itself and with the other tools. We will discover what we can learn about efficiency in the use of these tools, and how to take available information these tools provide and drive conclusions that are the basis of a well conceived marketing plan. In short, we are going to learn how to USE MARKETING instead of simply studying what it is. In the process, we will also learn, by default, what it is.

Marketing is more than definitions, abstract thinking, theory, and being a sales manager. It is a science that incorporates functional knowledge that operates, not in a vacuum, but based upon accepted principles. It is also more than studying independently identified courses in marketing such as a principles class, advertising, sales, marketing management, and consumer behavior.

Marketing requires something that threads the first course into the last course without being redundant. It can be compared to a surgeon who studies medicines, anatomy and the use of surgical tools. Sooner or later, we trust the surgeon-to-be will put all of these tools together prior to beginning his or her medical practice. The same is true of this integrated approach to studying marketing. We will build upon the knowledge gained and tools studied in one class taking them with us into the next class. This common thread will be studying the tools of the profession of marketing management. Decision-making will evolve from this study.

Principles of Marketing

Students must be functionally aware of four primary marketing tools:

A.   Essential Marketing Environments (**Threats** in the SWOT analysis)

B.   Product Demand Life Cycle (PDLC)

C.   SWOT analysis: Strengths, Weaknesses, Opportunities, and Threats

D.   Market to product or service conditions:

      1.   Existing product or service
      2.   Existing consumer base (all consumers within the industry)
      3.   New products or service
      4.   New consumers (new consumers to the industry)

Three Marketing Questions: The basis of all marketing discussion.

- Where Are We Now?
- Where Do We Want to Go?
- What is the Best Way to Get There From Here?

It is crucial to any situation in life to first determine where one is at before trying to go someplace else. This is true in personal relationships, driving to work or play, studying a college subject, going to an appointment or making marketing decisions in product development, advertising, distribution of products, and pricing of these products or services.

In a principles or introductory marketing course, we must try to answer the first question, **"Where are we now?"** The answer to this question is the foundation upon which we base or should base every marketing decision.

> **When addressing the marketing question, "Where are we now?" four primary marketing tools come to mind.**
>
> 1. Marketing Environments Analysis
> 2. Product Demand Life Cycle (PDLC)
> 3. Analysis of <u>S</u>trengths, <u>W</u>eaknesses, <u>O</u>pportunities, & <u>T</u>hreats (SWOT)
> 4. Product/Service Marketing Matrix.
>
>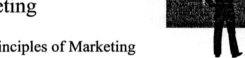
>
> Principles of Marketing

Have you ever tried to give someone directions to someplace without knowing from what direction they are coming? If they are on the phone the first thing we ask them is "Where are they now?" It is so obvious that we cannot give directions without first knowing this little detail.

The same is true in marketing. Unless we know something about our current situation, where we are, it is impossible to give good directions for getting to some place else. We can describe and define the intended destination all we want, but it is of little value in determining how to get there.

These four marketing tools answer the question, "Where are we now?" It is important to give directions beginning from a given point and going from one point to the next point. This is why we are addressing these tools in the order listed above.

We begin with a part of the situation analysis called an environmental scan. These environments have little to do with trees, water, fowl, fish and mammals, but are the environments in which marketers must function at home and abroad.

Three Primary Marketing Questions

- Where Are We Now?

- Where Do We Want to Go?

- What is the Best Way to Get There From Here?

Principles of Marketing (MKT111) students must be made functionally aware of four primary marketing tools;

A. Market Environments (Threats in the SWOT analysis)

B. Product Demand Life Cycle (PDLC)

C. Strengths, Weaknesses, Opportunities and Threats (SWOT) analysis and how this helps the marketing manager develop LEVERAGE (Opportunity).

D. Market to product conditions:
1. Existing product or service
2. Existing consumer base (all consumers within the industry)
3. New product or service
4. New consumers (new consumers to the industry)

Student Notes:

_____

_____

_____

_____

_____

_____

_____

_____

_____

_____

_____

_____

_____

_____

_____

_____

_____

_____

_____

_____

_____

The Market Environments

Look at the marketing Environments much like you would walking into a new class for the very first time. Where is everyone sitting? Am I early or late? Where do I look like I might fit in this class? What does the teacher look like? Is there anything on the board I should pay attention to? Do I have the same textbook as everyone else?

You ask yourself these and dozens of other questions. Why? You are doing a scan of your environment to see if and what adjustments you will need to make to fit into the class. We do the same thing in marketing. It is an environmental scan.

The marketing environments must all be considered even though some may not be a direct factor in the current analysis. Marketing environments are not circumstances that can be easily altered by the marketing department or a company, but are the circumstances within which they must operate.

Economic: Is our product affordable? Look at the market in which business will be done and see if there is an economic receptivity.

Economics includes many things. There are both the internal and external economics to consider. Internal economics include the financial situation of the company. External economics looks at the market place.

Social/cultural: Norms, subcultures, perceptions, status symbols?

Even though a product could be used by a society, will that society allow it to be used without sanctions? Might differentiation be based upon status? Religion? Social rules? Are some things this product offers a taboo? Is there something internal to the company social structure that could be a threat in production, manufacturing, selling?

Legal/political: Current or pending? Are the winds of opportunity blowing in the desired direction? All products are not equal according to local statutes and political influences.

Watch for pending legislation, changes in court structures, re-routing of traffic around your place of business. Has a recent election changed governing hands? Is there an influential element of society pushing for legislative change that could affect sales and distribution of your product or services?

Competitive: Direct? Indirect? Disposable Income?

Part of this marketing environment consideration includes an internal and external SWOT analysis. Evaluate the direct competition (hamburger with hamburger), indirect or substitutable competition (fast-food hamburger with sit-down restaurants), and disposable income or time. Too often we forget that consumers put a price on their time and budget it just like their money. If a product is going to require them to sacrifice time being used to do something else at present, to use the product, this limited disposable time may become a major threat.

Technological: Is this a potential factor? Can it obsolete quickly? Is automation a factor?

Technological threats can be both internal and external also. Efficiency comes from technology. Is your workforce capable of being trained? Will schooling be required of your work force? Does the competition have a competitive or absolute advantage in the use of technology? Web sites.coms? E-commerce?

The   Product Demand Life Cycle

The life of a product is a consumer demand curve. This curve increases as consumer demand for the product or service increase and drops off when consumers no longer need or desire the product. Business cycles depend more on how well management takes advantage of these consumer demands for a product. Let us clarify, through product categories.

There are three basic consumer products: Convenience goods, Shopping goods, and Specialty goods. Knowing the differences between these product types is critical to both the marketing manager and the ultimate consumer.

Convenience goods are products that consumers use or seek on a regular basis, have only a limited priority over competing products, do not require high-involvement shopping or comparing, and are usually purchased in spite of the sticker price. Convenience goods satisfy spur-of-the-moment needs or desires and tend to be consumed soon after being purchased.

Shopping goods are products that take a little more time to purchase. Price, style, brand, availability, choices and product knowledge all play a part in the consumer decision process. When consumer perceived value and price tag match consumer standards, they make a purchase. Price equals value.

Specialty goods are products for which consumers will not accept a substitute. Price is not an issue. If a substitute product is acceptable to the consumer, then the product, by virtue of the consumer behavior, has been down graded to a shopping item.

To handle these goods is a business decision. Consumer demand is a marketing issue. These are two different things.

Notes:

_____
_____
_____
_____
_____
_____
_____
_____
_____
_____
_____
_____
_____
_____
_____

Product Demand Life Cycle
Addresses the Marketing question, *"Where are we now?"*

Although the PDLC is divided into four, and sometimes, five stages, each stage is determined by the level of consumer demand.

The Product Life Cycle, as it is identified by many textbooks, is driven solely by consumer demand.

IT IS NOT A BUSINESS LIFE CYCLE!

Principles of Marketing - James W. Stark

The Product Demand Life Cycle (PDLC) is completely dependent upon the consumer and his or her demand for a given product/industry. This is not to be confused with any business cycle. If a business decides to handle an existing product, that does not move the product into the Introductory Stage. It simply means that the business is now making consumers aware THEY are handling this product for the first time.

The life of a product is 100% dependent upon consumer demand. There is little a business can do to extend the life of any product if consumer demand is not there. It is up to the marketing plan to build a strategy that will develop product appeal to identifiable market segments. As the product develops in the mind of consumers, and as more competition enters the market, targeted segments become more and more finite. Segmentation and niche marketing become the essence of the marketing plan.

A business life cycle, in contrast to the PDLC, is usually a management issue. A business must look at their market mix (a marketing issue), their product mix (a merchandising issue) and their operations (a business management issue). The four stages of a business cycle are recovery, peak, recession, and valley.

Business Life Cycle

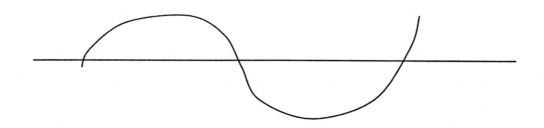

Product Demand Life Cycle

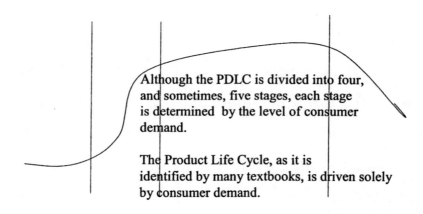

Although the PDLC is divided into four, and sometimes, five stages, each stage is determined by the level of consumer demand.

The Product Life Cycle, as it is identified by many textbooks, is driven solely by consumer demand.

IT IS NOT A BUSINESS LIFE CYCLE!

Principles of Marketing - James W. Stark

Characteristics of the Introductory Stage

Introductory
Stage

Principles of Marketing - James W. Stark

Notes:

_____
_____
_____
_____
_____
_____
_____
_____
_____
_____
_____
_____

- Consumers are unaware of this new product or service.

- There is NO DIRECT COMPETITION.

- This could be a new product or a new way to use an existing product or service (p/s).   Either way, consumer awareness is minimal.

- Competition at this level is over disposable consumer income.

- Consumers do not know how to use this new product or service, why they might need it, and depend on the sales person to advise them.

- Consumers are unaware of what problems the new p/s solves?

- Possible patents are pending or rights exist.

- No true market share yet exists.

- Price is not settled, but probably high in comparison to future pricing strategy.

- Consumers lack confidence (conviction) the p/s will do as it is purported.

- Large identifiable market segments, that will eventually use the product, have yet to try the new product or service for the first time.

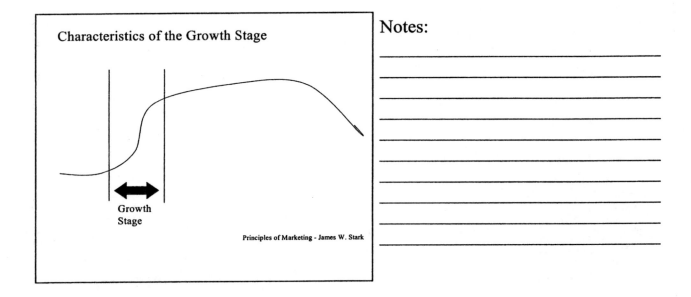

Characteristics of the Growth Stage

Growth
Stage

Principles of Marketing - James W. Stark

- The initial determining characteristic of the growth stage is the entry of competition as consumer demand is increasing (supply & demand).
- Consumer product awareness and understanding is increasing.
- Sales people still explain to the consumer product features and benefits due to the limited consumer product knowledge.
- New, more focused, markets begin to emerge.
- Competition is mostly direct and disposable income. Substitutable new products are not yet an issue.
- Product modifications begin to appear as unique consumer demands begin to be made and target groups become more homogeneous.
- No real market share exists, as yet, since large groups of identifiable potential and untapped markets still exist.
- Consumers are making their "first purchase" and have yet to judge on both their current and future need for the new product and their perception of the manufacturer or model.
- There is little variation in available models.
- Some product differentiation begins. Initially this differentiation is based upon function as cheaper models begin to find a market niche.
- Product KNOWLEDGE level of most consumers is limited, but is beginning to increase as more and more mainline consumer groups buy the product.

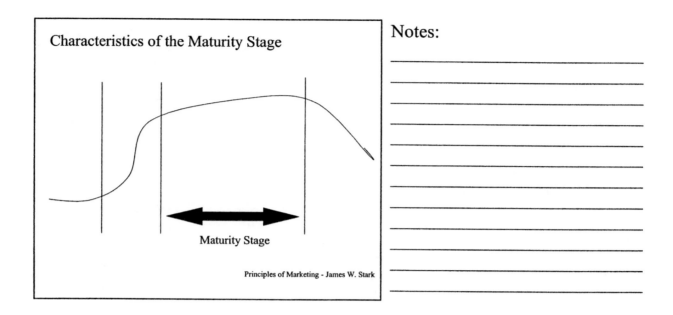

Characteristics of the Maturity Stage

Maturity Stage

Principles of Marketing - James W. Stark

Notes:

The maturity stage of product demand has several identifiable characteristics:

- There is significant market demand and first-time buyers are making their second or replacement purchase, be it an upgrade or newer model.
- Market share becomes an issue as consumers are declaring model preferences and brand loyalties.
- One company's growth is another company's loss (market share).
- Consumer groups rival the product knowledge of sales persons.
- The length of this stage depends upon fads, trends, consumer fickle and availability of resources.
- Few large groups of identifiable markets still exist. Most growth is based upon stealing market share.
- Competition is direct and substitutable, very stiff, and unforgiving.
- Product specific repair shops begin to open for business.
- Differentiation can come through correct use of any of the four Ps.
- Second half of the maturity stage brings in price differentiation issues.
- Later in the maturity stage competing products have the same consumer perceived features and benefits.
- Name brand is a major advertising differentiation.

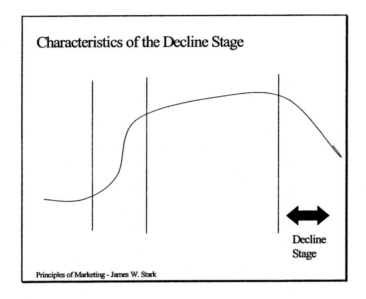

Characteristics of the Decline Stage

Decline
Stage

Principles of Marketing - James W. Stark

The decline stage begins when one of three things happens:

1.   The product or service is obsolete and replaced with something newer.

2.   The product no longer satisfies a consumer need.

3.   Some external force (marketing environment) changes the business environment.

- Antique speculators begin to emerge.
- All sales final is a standard measure for selling this product or service.
- Product repair shops now service all makes and models instead of just their own make and model.
- In some cases, the price begins to rise again.
- No new dealers open for business.
- Substitutable products have dealt the original product a severe blow.

This decline stage is not due to business failure, but to consumer demand failure. When consumers no longer see a product or service of value, businesses left handling this product will fail; too much supply and limited demand.

Marketing S.W.O.T. Analysis

(Where are we now?)

Looking at internal strengths and
Weaknesses and external opportunities
And threats

| Marketing S.W.O.T. Analysis | Notes: |

Marketing S.W.O.T. Analysis

Assessment of a product's unique features and benefits, position in the Product Portfolio model, and marketability.

- Where, in the eyes of the consumer, is this product on the Product Demand Life Cycle?
- Product Portfolio Model: Dog? Star? Question Mark? Cash Cow? Building strategy in applied or marketing management?
- What are the strengths of our product versus those of the competition? Differentiation?
- Barriers to entry?

Principles of Marketing - James W. Stark

Notes:

_____

_____

_____

_____

_____

_____

_____

_____

_____

_____

_____

_____

There are three ways to look at a SWOT:

1. Internal Strengths and Weaknesses; External Opportunities and Threats.

   - This is the definitional way marketing has been taught in the past.

2. Competitor Strengths and Weaknesses; Their Opportunities and Threats.

   - This is often done by consumer research and general knowledge.

3. Our product <u>S</u>trength Plus the competitor's <u>W</u>eakness equals <u>O</u>pportunity. Threats come from the marketing environments.

   - This is where advertising leverage messages are built. If product X can do something that competitor product Y cannot do, and it is important to the consumers, advertise it as so.

It is crucial to be aware that one shoe does not fit all markets. Each market we can identify that has a different need becomes a different target market (TM) and another advertising campaign. Finding and sorting through these different needs and a product's ability to satisfy these needs is the end result of a good SWOT analysis.

Notes:

_____
_____
_____
_____
_____
_____
_____
_____
_____
_____
_____

One good way to determine strengths (and weaknesses) is to do a gap analysis looking for gaps between product claims and consumer perceptions. The control question is, does perception and reality match? PV= $. Does perceived value equal the price tag?

Possible causes of gaps include:

1. Strategic plans and actual tactical efforts in effect do not coincide.
2. Advertised benefits and product benefit delivered.
3. Management's purported strength and actual delivery of service.
4. Consumer expectations and actual delivery.
5. Wrong comparison with competitor products.

Product strengths are something one product does that the competition does not do. When a product's strength is matched by the competition it is no longer seen as product strength. What was once the strength of one product has now become a consumer benchmark for similar products. Simply being "as good as the industry leader" is not a compelling reason for markets to switch from their preferred brand to another brand or product.

```
┌────────────────────────────────────────────┐
│                                              │
│       Marketing S.W.O.T. Analysis            │
│              WEAKNESSES                      │
│   • Is product positioning a factor in the eye of the consumer? │
│   • Has product differentiation become a consumer issue?        │
│   • Does the market mix need attention?                         │
│   • Wrong package or content size for the intended TM.          │
│   • Distribution is not central to the intended TM.             │
│   • Obsolete?                                                   │
│   • Product/service isn't user-friendly?                        │
│   • Product/service addresses wrong consumer need.              │
│                                              │
│             Principles of Marketing - James W. Stark │
└────────────────────────────────────────────┘
```

Areas of concern may be repeated complaints from customers regarding a product feature, service, or some gap between perception and reality. The real concern at this point is whether the competition can or will take advantage of this weakness, whether it matters with the existing TM, or whether someone's research is getting the correct answer to the wrong question(s).

The above is true of any product and competing products. Any weakness can create leverage for the other. Monitor these issues for potential gaps on a continuing basis. Defend your own product weaknesses and take advantage of the competition's product weakness(es).

Is your distribution system what it should be? Are there financial or credit issues? Do you know where on the product demand life cycle the product is located? Have you correctly identified who the competition really is? Do you understand what industry it is into which your product falls?

_____
_____
_____
_____
_____
_____
_____
_____
_____
_____

Marketing S.W.O.T. Analysis
OPPORTUNITY

- This is where some text books get it wrong. Opportunity is not only an internal analysis, it is an external leverage consideration.
- **S** (your product) +**W** (competitor) = **O** (opportunity); **S+W=O (leverage)**
  - One product's strength plus the weakness of the competitor's product equals opportunity or leverage.

Principles of Marketing - James W. Stark

One product's strength PLUS the weakness of the competitor(s) product equals opportunity. **This is known as leverage**. Opportunity can be determined by first knowing what one is capable of doing that the competition is not currently doing or is doing poorly.

Competitor barriers to entry become important defensive and offensive factors during this stage of S.W.O.T. Try to leverage first in the area of greatest barrier to entry for the competitor. The greater the barrier to entry or duplication, the less likely the competitor will try to duplicate your product's strength.

A price discount can be duplicated in a short time period by the competition. True barriers to entry leverage require the competition to build a new plant, establish other distribution facilities, or upgrade technologically. These take time to duplicate giving the competitor with the product strength time to exploit this strength with the consuming public.

Marketing S.W.O.T. Analysis
THREATS

- Threats are external to the organization and are not easily controlled. Each one of the marketing environments are potential threats to a product or service:
  - Economics, society, culture, legislation, politics, technology, competitive strategies.
  - Internal threats can be management skills, experience, R&D, resources, efficiency, but are usually looked upon as weaknesses.

Principles of Marketing - James W. Stark

Notes:

_____
_____
_____
_____
_____
_____
_____
_____
_____
_____
_____
_____

Marketing threats, outside operational factors, include all of the marketing environments discussed earlier. A threat can be the reverse of a SWOT advantage or leverage. That is, a given product's weakness and a competitor's strength becomes a threat, therefore, leverage to the competitor. Competition is one of the external environments.

Marketing options include taking either the offensive or defensive position. Do we protect our existing customer base, attempt to establish new target markets, sell a new product or product line to our existing market base, or steal market share from any combination of competitors?

Marketing **threats** are those things over which one has little control. Decisions are influenced by these threats and accommodations must be made. Ignoring these threats, a business decision, can be fatal to a company or operation.

The Marketing
Product-Service Matrix

Market Product/Service Matrix

Current P/S

	Current P/S	
Current P/S Users	**Concentrate on Differentiation. SWOT analysis.**	Current product or service refers to the product, as originally promoted in the Introductory Stage of the PDLC.
	Current product or service users are those people who make up the entire market for a given product industry (pizza, cellular phones, fast-food) from which business market shares are derived (Pizza Hut, ATT, McDonalds).	

Principles of Marketing - James W. Stark

Current product or service users are those consumers who make up the entire market for a given product industry such as pizzeria, cellular phones, or fast food. From these industries individual business market shares are derived (Pizza Hut, ATT, McDonalds).

Current product or service refers to the product, as functionally promoted in the Introductory Stage of the PDLC. This condition, existing or current users and current product, exists primarily in the maturity stage of the PDLC. Until consumers begin to declare brand loyalties and preferences, true market share ownership does not exist for this product.

> NOTE: Individual/business consumer target markets cannot yet be identified as faithful to someone's share of market. One purchase by a customer does not make them a faithful consumer. It is the second buy that declares this consumer as someone's share of market.

This condition of existing consumers and existing product or service, is a maturity stage situation. Most of the consumers who will use this product have been identified and are declaring brand loyalties. This means, under these market conditions, the marketing department has few strategic options; steal market share, find ways for product improvement or defend their existing customer base.

A SWOT analysis does well at this point in time. Consumers are familiar with the product industry and significant competition exists. This means consumers have probably made a choice of brands or product and will repeat making the same purchase unless compelled to switch.

Product improvement means improving the product itself by differentiating it from the competition. In the SWOT we studied that leverage or opportunity is taking advantage of a competitor's weakness. How can we differentiate our product in such a way that the consumer will switch from their current brand of choice to our product or service?

Don't be different for the sake of being different, however. The difference has to address a consumer problem and solve it. **Consumers won't buy products; rather they buy solutions to problems.** They also don't switch brands unless the difference solves a consumer problem better than does their current brand.

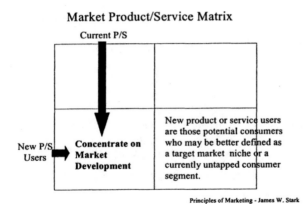

Market Product/Service Matrix

Principles of Marketing - James W. Stark

New product or service users are those potential consumers who may be better defined as a target market niche or a currently untapped consumer segment. In Consumer Behavior we learn about the consumer adoption process. Included in this marketing condition are finding additional uses for an existing product. Truly new consumers may then be identified.

An example of this is Arm-n'-Hammer Baking Soda. Originally a product used exclusively as a baking ingredient, it has found additional consumer uses in toothpaste and as an odor-absorbing agent.

This marketing condition exists primarily in the late Growth Stage and early Maturity Stage of the Product Demand Life Cycle if it is a new consumer niche being sought. It is in the Introductory Stage of the PDLC if the new customers have never heard of the product before and require significant instruction on how to use it and what it does as a problem solver.

Market Product/Service Matrix

New P/S

	Concentrate on Product Development:
Current P/S Users →	
	New product or service refers to a product, in the Introductory Stage of the PDLC, that can be used with, as an accessory to, or compliments the current users of a given product.

Principles of Marketing - James W. Stark

Current product or service users are those consumers who make up the entire product industry of users, usually displayed as the entire pie graph and from which business market share and segments are then derived.

New product or service refers to a product in the Introductory Stage of the PDLC, which can be used with, as an accessory to, or compliments the current users of a given product. The introductory stage is usually quite short as current users see these product and service types as complimentary to an existing product or service with which they are already familiar.

Strategy developed from this position in the market place will be to use an existing database of names and addresses to sell the New Product or Service. These consumers may be identified as the MOST LIKELY TO USE a new product of this type; i.e. Ice skaters (existing product: skates) are likely to become inline skaters (New product: inline skates). This is new product development. Discuss the product, not the users. They know who they are.

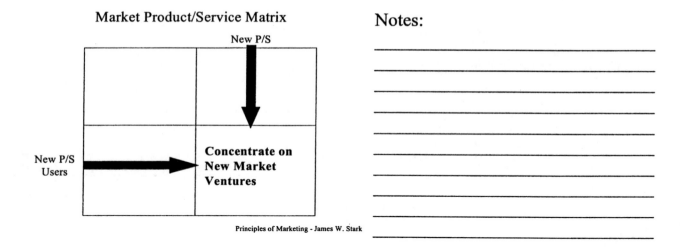

Market Product/Service Matrix

Principles of Marketing - James W. Stark

New product or service and new consumers mean this product is in the Introductory Stage of the PDLC. Consumers see the product as completely new. Their level of product understanding or knowledge is minimal, at best. This is called diversification. It is often a new market venture. Simultaneously as a company is trying to establish a base consumer group, they are promoting a product of which few consumers are presently aware or understand.

Strategy developed from this position in the market place will be to create a broad-based consumer awareness and understanding of the functional purposes of the new product. At the same time, try to establish who will be the primary target market. The advertising tends to be more generic and descriptive in nature in the early promotions

The goal, under this market condition, is to establish what the product is for and who is most likely to demand the product. Information is functional.

Sales and Advertising

The following presents the marketing decision making tools essential to the development of advertising and sales messages and strategies that correspond with the marketing tools taught in Principles of Marketing.

Although these tools can be taught independent of the principles of marketing tools, they are critical to teaching the Core Competencies
for a **marketing student** in a sales or advertising class. This includes:

1. The Advertising Pyramid
2. Messages appropriate for different stages in the Product Demand Life Cycle (PDLC).
3. Advertising strategies based upon the PDLC.
4. Product and price differentiation during the maturity stage of the PDLC.
5. Differentiating messages to specific niche target markets.

Advertising Pyramid

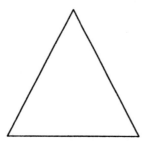

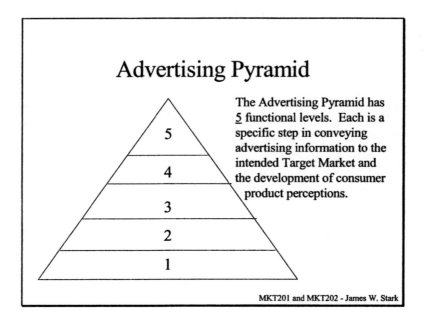

As with any building project, one must begin with a foundation upon which to build a structure. Marketing plans, product perception, or consumer's desire for a product or service require the same foundation upon which to build sales. Any consumer must be looked at as a building project. This means they must possess basic knowledge before they are ready for more complicated information or making decisions without guidance.

All purchase decisions, right or wrong, are based upon a basic consumer need. Consumers will only buy what they see as a solution to a personal problem. No matter how good the price, no desire to buy a product can exist if the consumer does not recognize the product or see it as a solution to a problem.

This is the premise of the Advertising Pyramid. Once a lower building block is in place, the consumer is ready for the next step.

Advertising Pyramid

```
        /\
       /5 \   DO NOT SKIP ANY LEVELS
      /----\  AT THE RISK OF A WEAK
     /  4   \ ADVERTISING CAMPAIGN.
    /--------\
   /    3     \
  /------------\
 /      2       \
/----------------\
/       1         \
```

MKT201 and MKT202 - James W. Stark

Student Notes:

_____
_____
_____
_____
_____
_____
_____
_____
_____
_____

Skipping any level(s) of the advertising pyramid is likely to be to a short cut to failure. Consumers have thousands of products and services seeking their disposable income and time. Usually an ad of any type has less than three seconds to gain a consumer's attention. This is true be it a television or radio commercial or printed advertisement. Little can be left to chance.

A consumer must have a basic understanding of a product's problem solving potential. S/he will have little time or interest in trying to figure it out for her or him self on the spot. Most consumers will simply move on to the next product or service that attracts their attention.

Leaving out any lower level of the advertising pyramid reduces the possibility of consumer desire for the product. If we don't understand something, we move on to something else that demands our time, energies and money.

Advertising Pyramid

```
        /\
       /5 \    Each step may, in fact, be a part of
      /----\   an over all advertising campaign,
     / 4    \  with each step having its media
    /--------\ moment!
   /  3       \
  /------------\
 /   2          \
/----------------\
/      1          \
/------------------\
```

MKT201 and MKT202 - James W. Stark

Step One:	Create an awareness of the new product or service.
Step Two:	Help consumers understand what this new P/S will do. Usually this is descriptive in nature and rather generic.
Step Three:	Show convincing evidence the product or service will perform as purported.
Step Four:	Personalize the message to targeted groups of consumers allowing them to now internalize the information. Benefits – Benefits – Benefits!
Step Five:	Hire personnel to run the cash registers.

Each step in the advertising pyramid is crucial to developing of a repeat customer. Individual steps in the advertising pyramid can be a different component of the overall advertising campaign. We begin with a broad base appeal (Step One in the advertising pyramid and diversification in the Market Product-Service Matrix). As we move up the advertising pyramid, our primary target markets become clearer as will the targeting of our advertising messages.

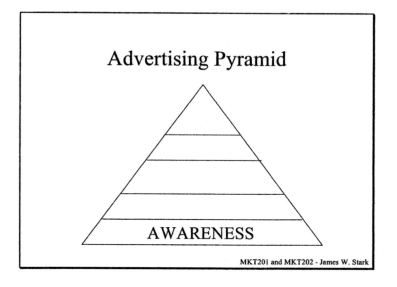

Advertising Pyramid

AWARENESS

MKT201 and MKT202 - James W. Stark

MKT201 and MKT202 - James W. Stark

Notes:

_____

_____

_____

_____

_____

_____

_____

_____

_____

_____

_____

The foundation is the knowledge that the product or service exists. One does not have to understand much at this point. The purpose of initial advertising is to get the name of the product out to the consuming public. Make the name a household word. This is the curiosity that kills the cat…that is, we are trying to set the stage for that curiosity.

AWARENESS LEVEL

- Introduce the new product or service to the general or targeted market.
- Talk about the product itself, not the user of the product. Develop functional knowledge.
- Attempt to elevate the name of the product to the level of a household word.
- Consumers may not be sure who would be the primary user of this new product or service at this point in the advertising schedule.

MKT201 and MKT202 - James W. Stark

Advertising Pyramid

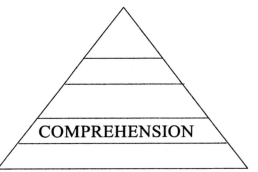

COMPREHENSION

MKT201 and MKT202 - James W. Stark

Comprehension or understanding has more to do with addressing the purpose for which the product or service has been made available. This is NOT THE TIME to make the consumer understand s/he needs the product. In other words, discuss what the product does, not "this is for you." This is product development! We discuss consumer/product comprehension at this point in the advertising campaign.

COMPREHENSION LEVEL

- This level is still primarily product introductory information.
- The information helps the potential consumer understand what problem(s) this new product solves.
- As with the awareness level, this information is external to the decision making process of the consumer.

MKT201 and MKT202 - James W. Stark

Advertising Pyramid

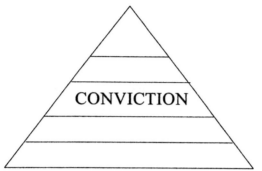

MKT201 and MKT202 - James W. Stark

Student Notes:

_____
_____
_____
_____
_____
_____
_____
_____
_____

Conviction is not persuading individual consumer s/he needs the product, but providing evidence that the product will perform as it is purported to do. As far as the consumer is concerned, at this point in his or her life, s/he now knows the product exists, understands what problems it helps consumers solve, and has seen evidence that it actually solves the consumer problem.

If there is enough evidence to prove to the potential TM, evidence the product is for real, and the advertising message has made this point evident, the next step is to move from the external message to the internal message.

CONVICTION LEVEL

- Present documentation or physical evidence this product or service will deliver as purported.
- Convince the general consumer that this new product or service is of value to some one.
- Show value, not in dollars, but in Life Values.
- Begin differentiating from direct competition if any exists.

MKT201 and MKT202 - James W. Stark

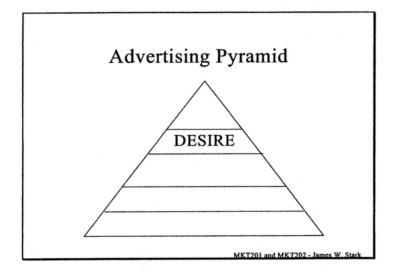

Advertising Pyramid

DESIRE

MKT201 and MKT202 - James W. Stark

It is time to get real personal with our advertising message. This is the point in advertising where one might say, "And we mean YOU!" Try to get the consumer to INTERNALIZE the advertising message. Since this is in the early stages of product development, price is only somewhat relevant. The consumer has little with which to make price comparisons, as there is little direct competition with similar products. Competition, up to this point, is over disposable income and time. Segment your primary target market with a primary message using a primary medium to reach them.

DESIRE LEVEL

- This is the first time the ad attempts to have the consumer internalize the information for personal use.
- Demonstrate specifics; i.e. specific problems for specific consumer types.
- Profile WHO THAT CONSUMER IS to help the intended target market identify with this product or service.

MKT201 and MKT202 - James W. Stark

Advertising Pyramid

```
        /\
       /  \
      /ACTION\
     /--------\
    /          \
   /------------\
  /              \
 /----------------\
/------------------\
```

MKT201 and MKT202 - James W. Stark

Notes:

_____
_____
_____
_____
_____
_____
_____
_____
_____
_____
_____

If the product or service has been properly introduced, correctly positioned in the minds of consumers as a problem solving product or service, and s/he has internalized the message, ACTION is the next step. **Caution: This step can mean acceptance OR rejection.**

There are other issues marketers must still concern themselves with including product/consumer usability, affordability, availability, and authority to buy (spend $$ for) the product. The ACTION level has two lives. One life is when early users and general consumers begin buying the product or service. The second life at the ACTION level of the Advertising Pyramid is when niche marketing comes of age in the Product Demand Life Cycle.

ACTION is the ultimate goal of any advertising campaign no matter where the product is located on the PDLC. A word of caution here…one advertising campaign cannot appeal to everyone's individual needs. Try to appeal to everyone and the advertising campaign will end up appealing to no one. Develop primary messages for targeted markets. Use a primary medium this targeted market is most likely to read, watch, see, or hear during the course of their daily living.

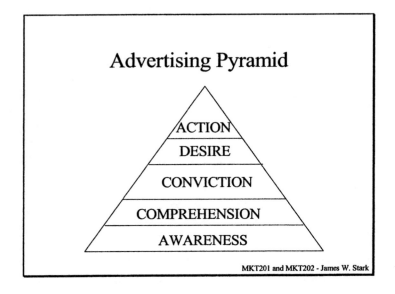

As the pyramid narrows, so does the identity or profile of the primary consumer. At the lowest level, that being the awareness level, the advertising message makes a broad appeal without discriminating (segmenting) markets. Many will hear, read, and see advertising messages, but not all will be viable consumers of the product or service.

Much like the building of a house, without a foundation, there is nothing upon which to build a solid structure. Without a solid broad based awareness and understanding of the product, consumers are not likely to seek additional information about the product. Without consumer conviction that the product will actually perform as it is purported, a desire for the product cannot be developed in the minds of consumers. ACTION (sales) will not happen. We can only see the ACTION by measuring sales.

This is much like the tip of the iceberg principle. We only see about 10% of the iceberg (ACTION) above the waterline. That means the 90% of the iceberg that is under the waterline is supporting the 10% that we see. This is just as true of an analogy in the advertising pyramid. We see the ACTION/sales, that which is above the waterline. Rob the advertising campaign of lower, any of the supporting levels, the 90% below the waterline, and the iceberg sinks deeper into the water; fewer sales!

Advertising and Sales

- Strategy is based upon consumer knowledge, product availability, and the consumer internalizing the primary message as personal and needed by him or her.
- Message emphasis is based upon where the product or service is in the consumer demand life cycle; i.e. Product Demand Life Cycle

---

Primary Message – Primary Target Market – Primary Media

If I said, "*All of the answers to every quiz in this course can be found on page 96 of this book,*" would you be interested? Of course you would. This is a primary message to a primary target market (TM). No one else is or will be interested in what may be on page 96. I also put this quiz message in THIS MANUAL. The manual is the primary medium for you, the primary TM. We now have a primary target market, message and medium.

An advertising or sales person must be able to identify who his or her TM is, and WHO IT ISN'T. Unless we know who is and who is not our targeted market, our message will be too generic. A generic message is an attempt to appeal to everyone and it will not work. No matter how good the product or service, there will be skeptical consumers and those who are not interested.

If one product can appeal to everyone equally, we would not need a variety of automobiles, textbooks, colleges, ice cream flavors, and/or friends. This is why the word PRIMARY is in the above illustration.

Understanding the Target Market.

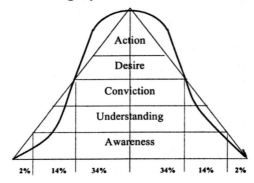

Advertising Pyramid & the Bell Curve

Action

Desire

Conviction

Understanding

Awareness

2% | 14% | 34% | 34% | 14% | 2%

MKT201 and MKT202 - James W. Stark

As with any statistical problem, there is always a centralizing tendency and not all potential consumers are within the apex, or umbrella of the curve. No one can sell a single product to everyone unless there is a monopoly. Even then everyone may not feel a need for the product or service.

Helpful to developing a good understanding of a target market is the statistical bell curve. Most consumers will develop an awareness of a product, fewer will understand what the product is intended to do, and even fewer will take the time to determine if the claims of the product are probable.

The Bell curve and Advertising Pyramid basically say the same thing. We start with a broad message and tailor it more to specific audiences as we move up the curve. At the peak we have our most dedicated customers.

68% of the total probable market in this example (DESIRE) is likely to consider purchasing and using the product or service. This is even narrower when developing market niches within targeted markets. This graph/tool overlay helps us understand that advertising and sales pitches are never going to have equal successes across all the consumer segments.

Developing Advertising Strategy Using The Product Demand Life Cycle

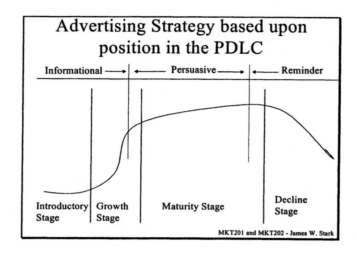

There are three basic advertising strategies:

1. **Informational advertising** informs potential consumers (Target Markets) of the existence of a new product, what it is capable of doing for the consumer, and some evidence it will do as purported. This is a must during the Introductory and Growth two stages of the PDLC. Manufacturers are not really sure who will ultimately become their market. Consumers are not certain if they are candidates for the product.

2. **Persuasive advertising**, used in the Maturity stage, goes beyond convincing a consumer s/he may need the product to make their life easier. It is time to tailor the advertising message and attempt to create a desire. Desire for a particular product (brand loyalty advertising) is now developed by groups of consumers who share or have homogeneous needs for which the product was designed to solve. The consumer makes a knowledgeable decision to purchase a particular competitive brand for a particular reason ($TM=A^4+D$); Target Market equals Abilities (<u>A</u>ffordability, <u>A</u>vailability, <u>A</u>uthority to buy, and <u>A</u>bility to use the product) plus Desire.

Consumers see a difference between competing products and purchase the one that best satisfies their need or requirements.

3. **Reminder advertising** is used after the public at-large is well aware of what the product is, what it will do, s/he has declared a brand preference or rejected the product outright, and no longer is in need of being convinced the product will or will not serve his or her specific purpose. By this time in the PDLC consumers develop an image of a specific consumer market when thinking of a particular brand of product. Whether or not he or she is a member of that consumer group is quite well understood and the product or service has become part of the environmental market…social/cultural norms.

> **Note: Each of the three advertising phases ends just prior to the next stage in the PDLC. This small segment or stage in the PDLC could be a very long span of time. This is particularly true near the end of the maturity stage of the Product Demand Life Cycle. A product can be in the reminder phase of the advertising, but still in the last part of the maturity stage.**

Advertising Strategy based upon position in the PDLC

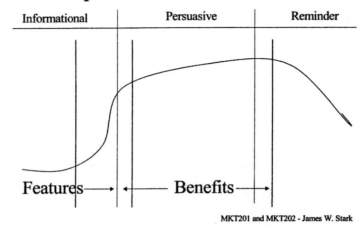

MKT201 and MKT202 - James W. Stark

During the early stages of the product demand cycle, consumers need information that will tell them about the new product or service. This information stresses the features of a product; i.e. product information. Although it is not a good practice to discuss a feature without making the bridge to the benefit of the feature, informational advertising tends to be feature driven. It tells the consumer about the product.

This usually means the potential consumer will inquire of a salesperson to explain product features when in the Introductory and the Growth stages of the consumer demand. When a product moves into the Maturity stage of the PDLC, the consumer has a better understanding of product features. Now s/he needs to have the differentiating benefits explained. Features equate to informational advertising as benefits equate to persuasive advertising.

In the informational stage we do more product development than market development as the product is lesser known or understood. In the persuasive stage we concentrate more on market (consumer) development, as consumers need to make a decision about personal use of the product. Both of these forces, features and benefits are going on all of the time. This helps the sales person or the advertising agent develop a message more fitting to the stage of the PDLC within which the product or service resides in the consumer's mind.

A reminder here is appropriate. The position of the product in the PDLC is consumer driven, not business driven.

Features are those bells and whistles that are identified as part of the product itself. Benefits are the result of using the product or service. Halogen lights on a car is a feature. The brilliance it gives to the road and the driver's ability to see at night is the benefit.

Notes:

_____
_____
_____
_____
_____
_____
_____
_____
_____
_____
_____
_____
_____
_____
_____
_____
_____
_____
_____
_____

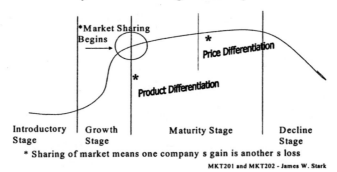

Using the Product Demand Life
Cycle for Message Development

*Market Sharing
Begins

*
Price Differentiation

*
Product Differentiation

| Introductory Stage | Growth Stage | Maturity Stage | Decline Stage |

* Sharing of market means one company s gain is another s loss

MKT201 and MKT202 - James W. Stark

In the maturity stage there are two different major types of differentiation. They are product and price differentiation. This can be consumer driven or marketing manager imposed. An advertising agency or a marketing manager can prematurely lower the price on a product in an attempt to steal market share.

If consumers perceive that there is little difference between competing brands, price will become the differentiating factor. Competitors will be forced to follow suite putting this product industry into the price differentiation side of the maturity stage and a pricing war erupts.

Example: Car rebates were intended to be a short-term program to attract new car buyers. Years later, rebates are still the norm. Auto manufacturers can't get rid of them. A strategic marketing decision made by a marketing manager, moved automobiles into the "pricing differentiation" of the PDLC. The second half of the maturity stage is where consumers are more price than product differentiation conscious.

Consumer perception moves a product along the line in the PDLC. When consumers fail to see much difference in product features and benefits, price becomes the predominant factor. This is particularly true when there are substitutable products or services that accomplish the same thing for the consumer. This has already happened when, several years ago, the only difference between models of cars became the front grill or ornament attached to it.

Only products that have captured a significant or prestigious image will be able to maintain higher prices. Competing products may seem similar, but the image that comes with owning a particular product has its price that some are willing to pay long after actual differences exist.

Market Share begins in the late growth stage and early maturity stage. For better understanding we put it between these two stages. This gives us the appearance of a pie graph. No company can claim share of market until there IS a share of market. Just because a first-time consumer of a new product purchases a particular brand does not mean s/he will be loyal to that manufacturer. The consumer's second-buy more likely determines brand loyalty, thus creating true market share measure.

Most competitors who are going to enter the market are in the market at this phase of the PDLC (Product Demand Life Cycle). Consumers are now knowledgeable about product features, functions and differences. Intentional product differentiation suggests that there are market choices (thus share). Large untapped homogeneous target markets no longer exist. Market niches become elements of every marketing plan. This means brand preference has been declared by consumers. This also supports the fact that true market share can now be measured.

Notes:

_____

_____

_____

_____

_____

_____

_____

_____

_____

Advertising Strategy
And the Advertising Pyramid

Advertising Strategies

- **Informational Stage provides:**

Conviction
Understanding
Awareness

MKT201 and MKT202 - James W. Stark

In the Introductory and Growth stages of the PDLC, large unique and identifiable segments of consumer target markets are becoming aware of the product or service, develop an understanding of what it supposedly can do, and are becoming convinced the product or service can actually do what it is purported to do. This is primarily informational advertising. It is information external to the consumer. S/he is gathering information that will eventually be part of her or his consumer decision process.

Without this basic understanding of a new product or service, the consumer is unlikely to ever compare his or her needs to the benefits of the product. At the same time, it is important for the marketing manager to realize a consumer can have a full understanding of the function and benefits of a product or service, be convinced it will do as purported, and still not declare him or herself a consumer of that product or service. Since a consumer has this option, it means information in the lower three levels of the advertising pyramid is external to the consumer. It is processed as INFORMATION. Individual consumer use of the product is only considered after having moved through these three lower levels of the advertising pyramid.

Advertising Strategies

• **Persuasive Stage provides:**

Action
Desire
Conviction

MKT201 and MKT202 - James W. Stark

In the late Growth and early maturity stages of the PDLC, large segments of consumers are now aware of the product or service, understand its purpose, and are convinced the product or service can actually do what it is claimed to be capable of doing.

Earlier consumers of the product, from back in the Introductory and Growth stages of the PDLC, are now knowledgeable enough about the product to give advice to fellow consumers. Sales people are no longer in as great a need to instruct the consumer while selling the product. Instead, they now fill orders to the specifications of the informed consumer. External information is now transformed to consumer benefits; information internalization begins. The consumer adoption process, as studied in consumer behavior, is traceable as consumers see personal and practical uses for the product or service in their own life situations.

The advertising messages takes on a different strategy; that of persuading consumers the product offered is better, cheaper, creates image or prestige, functionally different than is a competitor's product, more readily available, user friendly, or any other "leverage" one manufacturer may feel he or she has over the competition. This comes from doing a SWOT Analysis and looking at the market mix (product, pricing, distribution, and promo/advertising).

Advertising Strategies

- **Reminder Stage provides:**

```
        /\
       /  \
      /Action\
     /--------\
    / Desire   \
   /------------\
  / Conviction   \
 /----------------\
/ Understanding    \
/------------------\
/   Awareness       \
/--------------------\
```

When the general public is well aware of and has tried the product or service, and, substitutable products are readily available, advertising emphasis changes again. Reminder Advertising becomes the norm.

This can be as simple as a sign at an exit that states, "McDonalds, next exit. Turn left 3 blocks."

MKT201 and MKT202 - James W. Stark

Notes:

_____
_____
_____
_____
_____
_____
_____
_____
_____
_____
_____

In the late maturity stage, the marketing team must deployed a different advertising strategy...Reminder Advertising. In the introductory-growth stages of the PDLC, informational advertising is paramount. In the late growth stage and throughout the maturity stage of the PDLC, persuasive advertising is strategically employed. As we near the late life of a product demand cycle reminder advertising strategies are now used.

As a product or service nears the decline stage of the PDLC, ACTION is the essence of the Advertising Pyramid and message. Consumers are aware of the product, the competitors, and something new...the availability of substitutable products. In fact, there may be a product on the horizon that will eventually replace the current demand for the existing product. The price of the product in the reminder phase of the PDLC becomes pivotal to many consumer groups. Motel 6 does an excellent job of making price the issue when they run an advertising campaign pointing out that, when your eyes are shut, both the expensive motel room and Motel 6 look identical. The difference? You get change back at Motel 6.

A summary of the Advertising Pyramid and developing strategies from where the product or service is located on the Product Demand Life Cycle:

Advertising PDLC Strategies

- **Informational Advertising**
  - Creates awareness, comprehension and conviction during the Introductory and Growth stages of the PDLC

- **Persuasive Advertising**
  - Creates Desire for a particular product or service during the Maturity stage of the PDLC.

- **Reminder Advertising**
  - Used primarily during the late Maturity and early Decline stages of the PDLC.

MKT201 and MKT202 - James W. Stark

Student Notes

_____

_____

_____

_____

_____

_____

_____

_____

_____

$$TM = A^4 + D$$

The Formula for Developing Niche Markets and Targeted Advertising Messages

$$TM = A^4 + D$$

TM (target market)

A^4 : <u>A</u>ffordable, <u>A</u>vailable, <u>A</u>uthority to buy, <u>A</u>bility to use the product or service (p/s).

D: Desire exists to use the p/s.

NOTE: If all elements in the equation are in place, the consumer is an existing target market for someone; existing market share in the Market Product/Service Matrix

MKT201 and MKT202 - James W. Stark

Essential to tailoring a message to individual consumers is this advertising formula. Through research one will discover several reasons a particular group of consumers does not purchase a product or service. We have already discussed the Advertising Pyramid from which we introduce product information messages to the general public.

Now it is time to find and target niche markets. These are markets with unique product resistance or needs. It isn't the product itself, but something else that restricts them. The best opportunity (leverage/SWOT) can be determined by using the TM=A4+D formula. This is the next step, develop advertising messages that appeal to these unique market or consumer characteristics.

NOTE: The "**D**" in this formula is the same "**D**" that is found in the Advertising Pyramid, but is only one consideration in this message or strategy development formula. In the Advertising Pyramid, creating DESIRE is the singular goal.

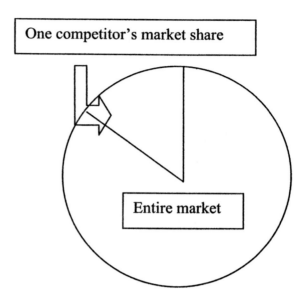

TM

(target markets)

MKT201 and MKT202 - James W. Stark

One competitor's market share

Entire market

The pie-graph to the right represents an entire market of which individual companies and name brands have a share of this market. A market is the entire graph, say those people who buy sports tennis shoes. Nike, Reebock or L.A. Gear will only have a share of that market. Each share represents a homogeneous group of consumers with a common problem THEIR BRAND solves for better than do the competitor brands.

The target market is that unique group of people with a homogeneous problem; a problem they share and the product offered or service can solve or satisfy their perceived need.

Target markets means there are also groups of consumers who are not part of the targeted market. If necessary, review the information provide earlier in this textbook covering market niches, new versus existing target markets, Advertising Pyramid and message strategy, advertising phases in the Product Demand Life Cycle, and using the marketing mix.

This formula is used in conjunction with, but is different than all of these other marketing tools and considerations.

$$TM = A^4 + D$$

Availability of product or service (p/s)
Affordability of product or service
Authority to buy p/s
Ability to use p/s

MKT201 and MKT202 - James W. Stark

_____
_____
_____
_____
_____
_____
_____
_____
_____
_____
_____

The intent of this formula is, through research, to discover which one of the elements in the formula that is missing in the consumer's perception of the product. It is wise to note that if two or more elements are missing in an algebraic formula, one cannot solve the equation. If one element is missing, we can solve for that equation. This is also true of consumers. If a particular group of people lack in two or more of these formula elements, they are not a primary target market. We cannot easily sell product to them for which we cannot solve a consumer resistance. If there is only one element missing, we can develop a message of appeal to that element and solve consumer resistance.

This is where we discover which element, in our formula, is the reason for consumer resistance to product adoption. Is it Product Availability? Affordability? Usability? Authority? Desire? Advertising messages or sales pitches can be developed around each formula element. It is critical to remember that, as in any algebraic equation, we can only solve for one unknown. If two or more elements to the equation are missing in the consumer, then they are not or are they likely to be an immediate purchaser of the product or service. Solve for one element at a time.

$$TM = A^4 + D$$

Desire for the product or service
must
also exist.

MKT201 and MKT202 - James W. Stark

Notes:

_____
_____
_____
_____
_____
_____
_____
_____
_____
_____
_____

Refer back to the notes on the Advertising Pyramid if "D" (DESIRE) is the reason for product-adoption resistance. When a consumer has disposable income, authority to buy, knows how to use a product, and where it is available, but still does not make a purchase, it must be DESIRE that is missing.

> **NOTE**: No one product can appeal to everyone. Nothing is sold until a problem is solved for the consumer. If the consumer does not see the product as solving a significant problem in his or her life, OR, other problems are greater at this point in his or her life, no sale can be made. Discover the problem, in the consumer's mind, or fire the customer and move on to the next candidate.

Desire can only exist if the consumer has personally moved through the first three stages of the advertising pyramid: product awareness, understanding, and conviction. Inversely, a consumer may have the desire for a product, but is lacking any of the four "A's". The product may not be available, affordable, useable, or require authority to purchase. In this scenario, the consumer DESIRES the product, but still will not or cannot make the purchase.

$$TM = A^4 + D$$

- Remember, in developing an advertising message from this marketing formula:
  - If all elements are in place, the consumer is already someone's customer.
  - Find the missing component with the desired Target Market and advertise to that need.
  - If two or more components are missing from this group of consumers, they are not a target market.

MKT201 and MKT202 - James W. Stark

Lets look at a pizzeria industry example of using this formula to develop business or marketing niches. Can do the same thing with other restaurants? Colleges? Cars?

Developing an Advertising Message or Niche using $TM = A^4 + D$

Availability of product or service

EG; Dominos Pizza (30 minutes or less)

Affordability of product or service

EG; Little Caesars Pizza (Pizza-Pizza)

Ability to use product or service

EG; Pizza Hut (Menu items and sit-down dining)

Authority to buy product or service

(Specialty brands)

There are particular needs of consumers to which these leaders in the pizzeria industry appeal. Taste may have less to do with it than does the occasion. Dominos appeals to delivery (availability), Little Caesars appeals to quantity (affordability), Pizza Hut appeals to usability in their sit-down establishment and extensive menu, and many of the smaller competitors Mom and Pop pizzerias compete over quality (authority to buy quality).

Applying Marketing:

The following marketing tools will aid the advanced marketing student in integrating tools learned in previous marketing classes such as Principles of Marketing, Sales, and Advertising.

These tools will help answer standard marketing questions like **"Where do we wish to go?"** and **"What are some ways of getting there from here?"** As in any formula, there should be no element left out of balance. This is also true in the proper use of marketing tools and developing strategies appropriate for intended target markets.

Case driven classes must integrate previously studied analysis and decision-making marketing tools. Then, students must practice or apply marketing techniques. These next pages are intended to help move the student from studying marketing in the abstract to the application . . . Applied Marketing!

$$P = A - D$$

P: Problem
A: Actual state-of-being
D: Desire state-of-being

MKT215 and MKT 291 - James W. Stark

Notes:

_____
_____
_____
_____
_____
_____
_____
_____
_____
_____
_____
_____

We studied earlier that nothing is sold unless a consumer problem can be solved. Before a problem can be solved, the consumer must perceive s/he has a problem that needs to be solved. Whether it is real or imagined is not relevant. Perception is everything to the consumer!

Consumers will consciously or subconsciously assign numbers to their every circumstance. It is part of a human being's nature to do an analysis of self, other's perception of them, and perceived needs comparing them with the value or utility received from buying and using a product.

On a plus/minus scale beginning with zero as neutral ground, consumers who assign a negative number to their needs begin shopping for ways to solve this negative feeling. If the number of their preferred or desired state-of-being is neutral, no action (remember ACTION in the advertising pyramid?) is considered necessary.

Advertisers and sales persons alike must try to discover a gap between a consumer's actual state-of-being and his or her desired state-of-being. If the gap cannot be discovered through personal assessment, then the burden of responsibility falls on the advertisement or salesperson to "point out" a gap the consumer may not have realized existed in his or her life; P=A-D. The more negative the number ($*A - **D = ?$) the greater the likelihood the consumer DESIRES a solution to their perceived need.

Too often in sales or advertising marketing people SELL THE OFFER or product instead of solving a problem (assuming a problem has been identified) with the ownership of a product or service. Problem discovery comes through pre-call preparation, interview or marketing research. This problem becomes the primary appeal for the message in any advertisement or sales call.

Remember sales folks, it isn't one's commission or making money that is the primary issue. It is the finding, then solving of a consumer problem that solves everyone's issue or concern including your commission. If the product is seen as the solution to a consumer problem, sales commissions follow suite.

* Actual state of the consumer

** Desired state of the consumer

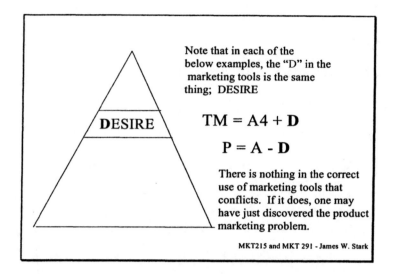

Note that in each of the below examples, the "D" in the marketing tools is the same thing; DESIRE

$$TM = A4 + D$$

$$P = A - D$$

There is nothing in the correct use of marketing tools that conflicts. If it does, one may have just discovered the product marketing problem.

MKT215 and MKT 291 - James W. Stark

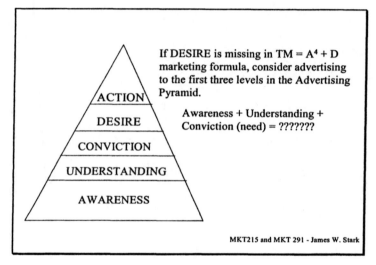

If DESIRE is missing in $TM = A^4 + D$ marketing formula, consider advertising to the first three levels in the Advertising Pyramid.

Awareness + Understanding + Conviction (need) = ???????

MKT215 and MKT 291 - James W. Stark

There is nothing inconsistent in using marketing tools correctly. They work together to help the marketing manager assess, interpret, analyze and develop proper strategy for the market in question. By integrating these tools, like the use of the tools in the carpenter's belt, and by using these tools for the job they were designed, we can draw conclusions upon which to build proper marketing strategy. If a conflict in tool uses is discovered, the problem with the marketing strategy may have also just been discovered.

Integrating the Advertising Pyramid and the Product Demand Life Cycle

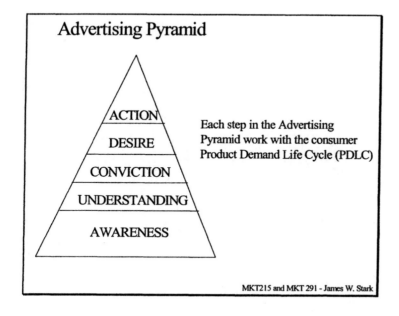

Advertising Pyramid

ACTION
DESIRE
CONVICTION
UNDERSTANDING
AWARENESS

Each step in the Advertising Pyramid work with the consumer Product Demand Life Cycle (PDLC)

MKT215 and MKT 291 - James W. Stark

Notes:

Another use for these marketing tools is the checks and balance that is offered by integrating the Advertising Pyramid with the Product Demand Life Cycle. Just as each step of the pyramid can be another message plateau for the advertisement campaign, advertising tactics change as we move along the consumer demand curve (PDLC).

There is no conflict here. If there is, then examine the possibility of the wrong advertisement message being used during a specific phase or stage of the product demand cycle. This is similar, in nature, to having the right answer to the wrong question. There may be nothing wrong with the advertising message, but it is either before its time or after the targeted consumers has moved on to other issues. Let's examine some of these messages and timing of them in the following pages.

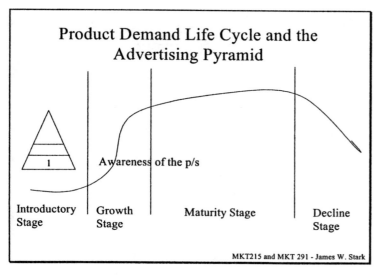

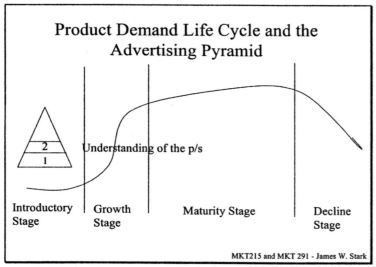

Several previously studied thoughts should come to mind as we look at these two graphs: There is limited competition. The competition that does exist is over disposable income and time of consumers. Informational advertising is paramount in the early stages of the PDLC. Large groups of potential consumers do not yet own this new product or service.

The Advertising Pyramid helps verify this marketing information. Now we know what to say and when it needs to be said in our advertising campaign.

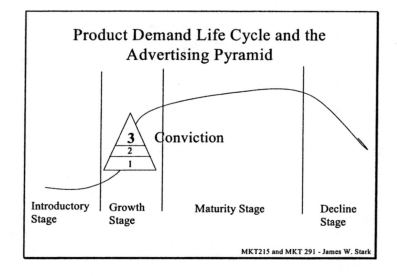

Notes:

_____
_____
_____
_____
_____
_____
_____
_____
_____
_____
_____
_____

In the growth stage of the PDLC, we apply the conviction message of the Advertising Pyramid. This consumer conviction comes from advertising information/evidence that the product is doing what it is intended to do…solve a consumer problem.

Competition is increasing because of consumer demand. Consumers will start to see differences in competing brands as we move up the growth stage on the PDLC. This difference may come in the form of product guarantee, store hours, distribution, product availability, service, or product design.

This means that the advertising message should start adding information about differences between competing products. The closer a product moves to the maturity stage of the PDLC, the greater some degree of differentiation is required. Consumers begin to declare brand preferences and loyalties. Conviction messages encourage the consumer to pick brand "A" over brand "B." These information messages must be well thought out.

Later we will see that the majority of probable consumers have tried the product during the growth stage of the Product Demand Life Cycle.

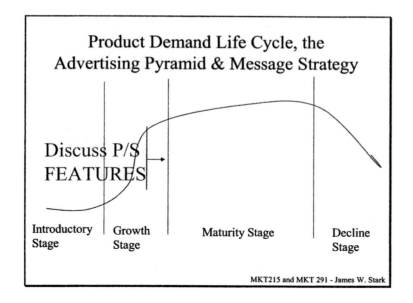

Notes:

_____
_____
_____
_____
_____
_____
_____
_____
_____
_____
_____
_____
_____

Discussing product information is the INFORMATION Stage of advertising. The advertising message here is simple: make the consumer aware of the existence of the new product or service, help the consumer understand what the product does as a consumer or business good, and explain the bells and whistles attached to the product or service being introduced. This falls into the Product Development, new customer quad of the Market Product-Service Matrix (more on this a little later in the book).

As will be introduced in Consumer Behavior, and as we have already alluded to in discussing the product demand life cycle, in the early stages of a product introduction, consumers adopt a product in stages or groups. Therefore, a broad base of consumers must be made aware of the product, what it does, and that it will perform to expectations. These are the first three levels of the Advertising Pyramid.

Provide information, external to the consumer, discussing features, explaining what a product does and show evidence that the p/s works.

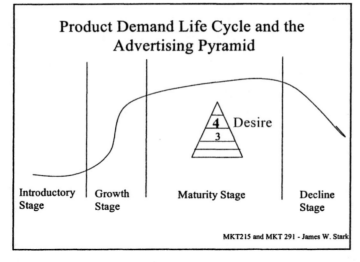

Product Demand Life Cycle and the Advertising Pyramid

4 Desire
3

Introductory Stage | Growth Stage | Maturity Stage | Decline Stage

MKT215 and MKT 291 - James W. Stark

Level four of the advertising pyramid is DESIRE. The lower three levels of the advertising pyramid are the central theme of advertising in the first two stages of the PDLC. Persuasive advertising messages become critical for developing desire for a specific product or brand name. Since consumers have, for the most part, declared brand loyalties by this time on the PDLC, differentiation is central to the advertising message by this time.

The differentiation may be in the 4 Ps of the market mix, the $TM=A^4 + Desire$ creating market niches, store image itself, the perceived actual state versus the desired state of the consumer, and/or personal image created by owning and using a specific product.

As we move to the right along the consumer demand curve in the maturity stage, price becomes more of issue, as products tend to begin to, once again, look a lot alike. When competition begins to enter the market in the late introductory stage and growth stage, there is little differentiation in the products. Consumers are not knowledgeable enough of the new product in the early stages to handle major differentiation. Therefore, marketers carry a message of general product awareness and understanding.

In the late growth and early maturity stages, differentiation is necessary. There is a fight over market share and consumers do not have the same perceived need for a product. One person may buy a computer to keep track of business records. Another may buy a computer to use it as a word processor and do school work. This is called product utility. Consumers buy the product that gives them the utility…differentiation.

In the late maturity stage, products again look a lot alike. Competition is the reason. One competitor develops a product difference using the SWOT analysis trying to create leverage. Competitors will duplicate the product modifications that consumers seem to desire. The difference is then nullified as all competitors adjust their product.

Eventually, most competitors have little upon which to differentiate other than image or price. Marketers should try to create the greatest barrier to duplication in their differentiation as possible. Do not make it easy for the competition to duplicate product changes and advertising leverage (SWOT).

Product Demand Life Cycle, the
Advertising Pyramid & Message Strategy

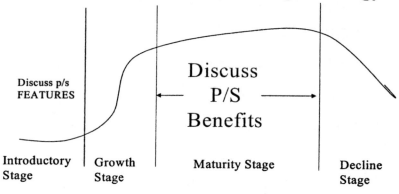

MKT215 and MKT 291 - James W. Stark

This is the Persuasive Stage of the advertising model. Where as earlier, the advertising message was one of basic information and understanding, now it is what the p/s does for the consumer. Being that this is the maturity stage of the PDLC, the advertising model says the advertisement must be persuasive. Products and services must be differentiated from one another. Market Share comes from persuading consumers to switch brand loyalties or chose one product over another. The advertising message must be more consumer-oriented and less product-oriented.

Value versus dollars becomes a significant issue with consumers in this stage of the PDLC. Similar to the scope of a rifle, two crosshairs are needed to site-in. Marketing looks at one crosshair as being the value of the product package as advertised and perceived by consumers. The other crosshair is dollars or cost to the consumer. This cost can be in real dollars or in opportunity cost. Benefits are what the consumer receives for using the product.

This can be demonstrated in another marketing word formula: ***PV=$** (Perceived value must equal the cost the consumer is willing to pay for the product).

Until perceived consumer benefits line up with the cost of buying or using a product, consumers will not make the purchase. The three most important issues of differentiation in the maturity stage of the PDLC… Benefits – Benefits – Benefits! Value – Value – Value! Utility – Utility – Utility!

*This word formula is a great reminder to marketing personnel that there is much more to determining the price of a product than profit margins. In the consumer's mind, value is not the price, but what s/he receives for that price. Opportunity costs may be an economic phrase, but it is very applicable to marketing and consumer mind-thought.

Consumers have thousands of other products and services vying for their expendable income and time. To go shopping for a product not only requires expendable income, but expendable time. Sorry folks, 10% off everything in the store just isn't going to line those consumers up at the cash register.

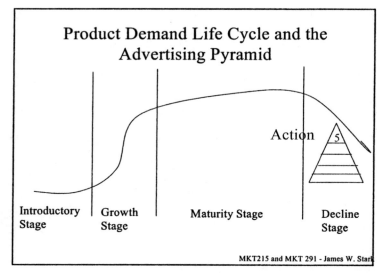

Product Demand Life Cycle and the Advertising Pyramid

Action

Introductory Stage | Growth Stage | Maturity Stage | Decline Stage

MKT215 and MKT 291 - James W. Stark

As discussed earlier, this is the reminder stage of advertising and ACTION is the only real emphasis in the advertising message. Consumer product awareness is across-the-board. Most differences in products are either eliminated or price driven. Consumers know quite well how to use the product and name recognition is very high. At this stage of the PDLC a simple reminder message will usually do the trick. An example of this might be an empty Coke bottle on a billboard. Very few people would fail to recognize it is a Coca-Cola bottle even if no words were included on either the bottle or the billboard.

In the very early stages of the Product Demand Life Cycle, competition is over disposable income and time as potential consumers are being asked to redirect their purchase dollars to a product they have not been previously buying. In the growth stage of the PDLC, direct competition becomes an issue.

Competitors jump in where profits, return on investments, are to be made. This is only natural in a free enterprise economic system. In the late maturity stage, substitutable competition becomes an additional issue or concern. Substitutable products present a possible threat to survival.

A factor that helps create the Decline Stage in the PDLC is the availability of substitutable products. Not only are there direct competitors, but indirect competitors. These substitutable (indirect competition) products broaden the product options available to the consumer.

When McDonalds first introduced "fast-food," there was no direct competition in the fast-food industry. Other restaurants existed, but these sit-down diners took time, time that many did not have for a lunch hour.

After McDonalds created, in the mind of lunch crowds, a great awareness and understanding of a fast-food industry, competitors jumped in like Burger King, Wendy's, and Mr. Quick's. Then, along came substitutable fast-food options in Taco Bell, KFC, and others who did not flip a burger as their main product offering to the consumer. One of the losers in the great competition over "the feeding of Americans" was and still is grocery stores.

The Wheel of Retailing is also a factor. This can be a marketer's nightmare. McDonalds has lost much of its original luster of being a limited menu, fast-food provider. Ray Crox, the founder of McDonalds, required meals to be served in 37 seconds to fit his concept of fast food. None of the original McDonald's had table service, or breakfast, lunch and dinner options on the menu.

As the Wheel of Retailing revolved, more items were added to the menu, table service became expected, and fast food at McDonalds almost became an item in history. Their inventory costs went up significantly as did the prices on their menu items.

A strange phenomenon may then occur in the decline stage of the demand for a specific product. Someone comes along and re-introduces the original concept of the industry's founding product. This does not send the product itself back to the introductory stage of the PDLC, but, in all fairness, the original product no longer resembles its original self either. So, McDonald's restaurant appearance has made room for Fast-and-Now hamburgers.

The Market Product-Service Matrix
Answering the Marketing Questions:

"Where do we want to go from here?"
"What is the best way to get there from here?"

Market Product-Service Matrix

	Current P/S	New P/S
Current P/S Users	This marketing tool helps the marketing manager answer the question, "*Where do we want to go from here AND what to do to get there from here?*"	
New P/S Users		

Given that the marketing question, "Where are we now," has been fully addressed using the PDLC, Environmental Scan and SWOT analysis, the marketing manager must address the second marketing question; "Where do we wish to go from here?"

The Marketing Product-Service Matrix explains the conditions that must exist and be considered to determine strategy. Does one wish to retain current market share? Steal market share? Develop a new product? Find a new target market? Diversify and find both a new product and market?

These are the only options available in the usual marketing situation. Develop a strategy by focusing on one of these options. We are finally beginning to see how these marketing tools can answer all three of the marketing questions posed.

Market Product/Service Matrix & Strategy

Current P/S | New P/S

	Current P/S	New P/S
Current P/S Users →	Market Share — Two Marketing Options exist if this is true: 1) Steal market share 2) Retain market share	
New P/S Users		

MKT215 and MKT 291 - James W. Stark

Strategy developed from these two existing conditions in the market place will require either offensive or defensive posturing. Defensive posturing means developing game plans designed to protect one's current share of market. Offensive posturing means developing game plans that are designed to:

a) Keep one's current share of market.

b) Steal market share from the closest competition.

c) Improve the product performance, availability, or price.

A current product and a current consumer base means that this product industry is well into the late phase of the growth stage or in the early maturity stage. Market share is usually well defined by this time. Large, identifiable new target markets or groups of consumers who have not at least tried the product some where along the line are difficult to find. Product differentiation is the marketing message and pricing of the product is critical. We are now in the upper levels of the advertising pyramid. Most of the consumer problems that the original product introduced to solve are now being solved.

Market Product/Service Matrix & Strategy

	Current P/S	New P/S
Current P/S Users		
New P/S Users	**Market Development:** Strategy is to find new uses and/or users of an existing product.	

MKT215 and MKT 291 - James W. Stark

Notes:

Notes:

_____

New product/service users are those potential consumers who may be better defined as a target market niche or an untapped consumer segment. They may also be a result of exporting the product. The current product, in its unmodified form and purpose of use, is general knowledge to consumers. The goal here is to find new users of the current product. Current product or service refers to a p/s that has been or is currently in use by at least one major segment of consumers.

Strategy:

Discover the reason the identified segment is not using the product and develop advertising to appeal to them ($TM = A^4 + D$). Arm and Hammer Baking Soda is an example of this strategy. Using an existing product, they **created a DESIRE** in new consumers to use baking soda as an odor-absorbing agent in kitchens, refrigerators, freezers, bathrooms, garbage, and garages, as a cleaning agent or toothpaste additive.

Emphasis is put on "MARKET (people) Development." The product is well beyond the introductory stage and consumers know it by brand name(s). Strategy is to find market niches or export the product. Develop consumers by identifying a use for the product that directly addresses consumer needs. Talk about, promote and profile consumer groups at this point in marketing message.

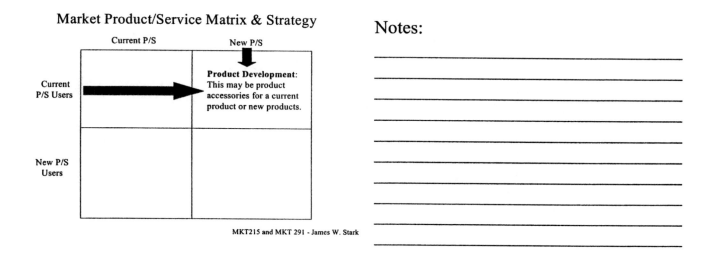

Market Product/Service Matrix & Strategy

Current P/S   New P/S

Product Development: This may be product accessories for a current product or new products.

Current P/S Users

New P/S Users

MKT215 and MKT 291 - James W. Stark

Notes:

Strategy developed from this condition in the market place is to use an existing database of names and addresses selling them the New Product or Service. These consumers may be identified as the MOST LIKELY TO USE a new product of this type; i.e. Ice skaters (existing TM) are also likely to be inline skaters (New product). Existing customers in the matrix are those who have a homogeneous consumer problem. This new product, such as a new type of cholesterol reducer that has not been on the market, may fit this existing market quite well.

Essential to the advertising campaign, at this point, is Product Development. Advertise product attributes creating product awareness and understanding in the mind of the consumer. Use the same marketing rules and principles as would be done for a product in the early stages of the PDLC. The advertising message is derived from the lowest levels of the Advertising Pyramid. The advertising message will be informational.

There is a good chance these consumers will have a short learning curve as they already are familiar with an associated product.

Market Product/Service Matrix & Strategy

	Current P/S	New P/S
Current P/S Users		↓
New P/S Users	→	**New Market Venture:** Marketing challenge is to find new consumers for a new product or service, both at the same time.

MKT215 and MKT 291 - James W. Stark

The most risky of all business ventures and marketing challenges is when trying to match new product with a new consumer. We may or may not have correctly identified the most likely consumer of the new product or service.

The marketing manager is trying to build advertising messages based upon lower levels of the Advertising Pyramid while trying to find the right group of people to which to advertise. This product is in the Introductory Stage of the Product Demand Life Cycle. All marketing principles apply for this stage of the product life cycle.

This is a good time to research why most new products fail. Even trying to find the best medium to carry the advertising message can present a challenge to the marketing manager. Find a primary TM, a primary advertising message target to that TM, and a primary medium to carry the message to this TM.

Integrating the Market Product-Service Matrix, The Product Demand Life Cycle And the Advertising Pyramid

Market Product/Service Matrix & the PDLC

	Current P/S	New P/S
Current P/S Users	1 Late Growth Stage & entire Maturity Stage of the PDLC	2
New P/S Users	3	4

MKT215 and MKT 291 - James W. Stark

Market Product/Service Matrix & the PDLC

	Current P/S	New P/S
Current P/S Users	1	2 New product suggests this will be the early stages of the PDLC; Introductory & Growth.
New P/S Users	3	4

MKT215 and MKT 291 - James W. Stark

By using these two different marketing tools we can verify the validity of the use of these tools and the information they provide us. The Marketing Product-Service Matrix gives us four separate but paired market situations: existing market, new market, existing product, and new product. By pairing up these circumstances, the matrix tells us what to do under any combination of these situations.

The Product Demand Life Cycle explains the consumer product demand. If when comparing these two separate tools, our results match, then the correct strategy is being used. What we look for when comparing or integrating these tools is conflicts in what they tell us. Corrective measures will be called for, but now we know what they are.

Let's assume that we think we have a condition such as exists in quadrant one above; i.e. an existing TM and an existing product. Then, using the PDLC marketing tool we determine that consumer demand is in the late maturity stage. We now know that in our advertising to these current customers, persuasive rather than informational advertising is the driving force.

Market Product/Service Matrix & the PDLC

Current P/S   New P/S

1	2
Current P/S Users

3 Late Growth and early Maturity Stages of the PDLC; Often used to develop Market niches.	4
New P/S Users

MKT215 and MKT 291 - James W. Stark

Market Product/Service Matrix & the PDLC

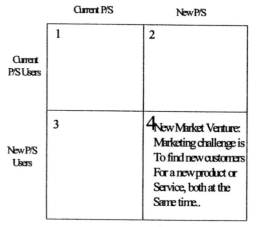

Current P/S   New P/S

1	2
Current P/S Users

3	4 New Market Venture: Marketing challenge is To find new customers For a new product or Service, both at the Same time..
New P/S Users

MKT215 and MKT 291 - James W. Stark

On the previous page, we validated our information by integrating our marketing tools. Similar to a carpenter using the square to validate how square a wall is before attaching a squared kitchen cabinet to it.

Let's again see how well these two tools square up to each other validating or denying our marketing strategy. In quadrant three above, the matrix shows that we have two market conditions: new product users and existing product. Our PDLC research shows that industry consumer demand is growing but we have been using persuasive advertising messages. OOPS! We are using the wrong advertising message. According to the PDLC, we should be using INFORMATION not persuasive advertising under these conditions.

This is the beauty of learning and understanding how each marketing tool works by itself and in conjunction with the other tools. With the power and knowledge of integrating the Product Demand Life Cycle and the Market Product-Service Matrix, the marketing manager is able to make some important marketing decisions. We can answer all three marketing questions: "Where are we, where do we need to go and how to get there from here?"

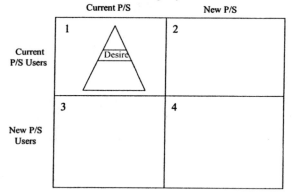

Market Product/Service Matrix & the Advertising Pyramid

MKT215 and MKT 291 - James W. Stark

If marketing plans are being made for conditions that exist in the upper-left quadrant of the Marketing Product-Service Matrix, advertising will center on creating consumer DESIRE for the product or service. Consumer perceptions have been established as this product or service (P/S) is in the late growth and early maturity stage of the Product Demand Life Cycle. Consumers are well aware of what the p/s does, who might be the primary user(s), and if the p/s delivers on its promise(s).

Product demand has been divided into market shares. Each market share exists because of unique product strengths that are attributed to that particular product or brand. Most consumer groups have been tapped and have tried the product. We are high on the Bell Curve. The strength attributed to a product has a group of consumers who see this strength as THEIR REASON, or centralizing tendency, for buying this product.

Consumers know who are and are not primary customers. The concern here would be if the marketing department recognizes the same thing? This is another excellent time to use the SWOT analysis tool to determine product strengths and weaknesses. A marketing manager may also us a focus group to help determine consumer perceptions of competing product strengths and weaknesses.

Market Product/Service Matrix & the Advertising Pyramid

Current P/S   New P/S

	Current P/S	New P/S
Current P/S Users	1	2 (Conviction / Understanding / Awareness)
New P/S Users	3	4

MKT215 and MKT 291 - James W. Stark

If plans are being made for marketing to the upper-right (Product Development/ Existing Consumer) quadrant of the Marketing Product-Service Matrix, the lower levels of the advertising pyramid become essential advertising messages. These consumers may be a fast-learn as they may already be familiar with an associated product or service, but not with this NEW P/S.

In this Product Development quadrant of the Product Marketing Matrix, consumer target markets must, once again, be made aware that the new P/S exists, understand it's purpose, and be convinced it is both worth their while to make such a purchase and it will perform as purported. What makes it worth their while? If the New P/S solves a consumer problem currently going unsolved (P = A - D); the consumer's desired state of being is greater than his or her Actual state of being.

Either way, the marketing manager has an existing customer base with homogeneous problem(s) who are likely candidates for a new product to solve the problems in common to this group of consumers.

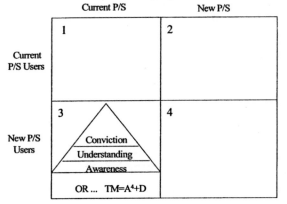

Market Product/Service Matrix & the
Advertising Pyramid

MKT215 and MKT 291 - James W. Stark

In this market situation we have an existing product in search of new users or consumers.

Once again we can use our Advertising Pyramid tool, but this time we discuss consumer instead of product use issues. Make the consumer aware of their need by profiling the consumer in the promotions. The TM=A4+D formula is also effective here.

When marketing plans are being made for the lower-left (New Target Market/Existing Product) quadrant of the Marketing Product-Service Matrix, the lower levels of the advertising pyramid once again become essential for developing targeted messages to this consumer.

These consumers are either a homogeneous or heterogeneous consumer group. If homogeneous-based, the consumer may be somewhat aware of the P/S, but has not used it in the past for multiple personal reasons. The P/S may not have been available in his or her area before. It may not have been affordable or s/he lacked ability to use it, or, authority to buy it. This consumer is similar (homogeneous) to the current or existing users of this product, but missing one of the elements in the $TM=A^4+D$ marketing formula.

If heterogeneous-based, the consumer is different in nature than previous P/S users and must be made aware that this product is also for them. It can solve THEIR consumer problems. Again, an example of this may be Arm and Hammer Baking Soda. It is an existing product (baking), but now has other (deodorant) uses, therefore, other (heterogeneous) users. The product characteristics have not been altered, but it has additional uses. Either way, the marketing manager has an existing P/S seeking new users.

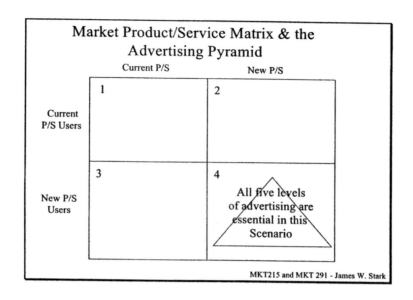

If marketing plans are being made for the lower-right quadrant of the Marketing Product-Service Matrix, each level of the advertising pyramid becomes essential as an advertising message. Begin with the lowest level. The product or service is in the introductory stage of the PDLC, it has yet to see any direct competition, and consumers may or may not accept this product or service as a solution to an existing consumer problem.

The competition that does exist is over disposable income and time. Information advertising is the way to bill your promotion and be prepared to create barriers to entry for future competitors seeking the same profit margins. When competition does come along, after your product has proven there are profits to be made watch for patent violation. Early competitors will try to duplicate what your product does as consumers have demonstrated enough interest to start making purchases.

Refer back to the PDLC section for what to do in this marketing situation.

The Product Portfolio

"Determining what to do with existing products"

(How to get there!)

The marketing department must eventually address the question, "Where do we wish to be or go from here?" Once a thorough situation analysis and assessment has been done, this question almost answers itself. A helpful tool for analysis of existing products has been developed by the *Boston Consulting Group. It is called the Product Portfolio.

This tool helps the marketing manager address the question about existing products and product lines, those that have been on the market for some time, and those that have recently come out of Research and Development. The Boston Consulting Group (BCG) refers to these products as Stars, Questions, Cash Cows and Dogs.

Developing Product Strategy for an existing product or service by using the *Product Portfolio approach. This helps answer the third marketing question.

Services

Products

MKT215 and MKT 291 - James W. Stark

One of the key responsibilities of a marketing manager or small business owner is to recognize the consumer value of the products s/he may have on the shelves at the store or place of business. Each product is a member of a product industry and each industry has a life or consumer demand curve. Products and services must fall under the examining eye and scrutiny of the marketing manager as to their current and future value and merit.

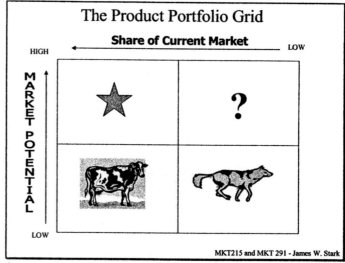

The Product Portfolio Grid

Share of Current Market

HIGH ← → LOW

MARKET POTENTIAL

HIGH

LOW

MKT215 and MKT 291 - James W. Stark

(The Boston Consulting Group)

Much like the Market Product-Service Matrix, the Product Portfolio aids the marketing manager in his or her processing and thinking through market situations. "If this is true and this is true, then . . .!"

This is process thinking. We assume very little and no one is interested in simply our opinion. Marketing managers must support their conclusions with tools of the profession. Anyone can have an opinion, even an opposing opinion. Usually these opinions are base upon bias, personal agendas, ambition, or ignorance of all the facts.

No marketing decision should be made in a void. This is also true about understanding and using marketing tools. Marketing tools, much like the tools of a carpenter, work in concert with one another. The integration of the marketing tools helps drive conclusions, develop marketing plans and do accurate situation (case) analysis. The result is process thinking.

Let's first examine the integration of the Product Portfolio model with the Product Demand Life Cycle. We will see if there is model conflict or coordination.

Remember that the Product Demand Life Cycle is completely dependent upon the consumer and his or her demand for a given product/ industry. This is not to be confused with any business cycle. If a business decides to handle an existing product, that does not move the product into the Introductory Stage. It simply means that the business is now making consumers aware THEY are handling this product for the first time.

The life of a product is 100% dependent upon consumer demand. There is little a business can do to extend the life of any product if consumer demand is not there. **It is up to the marketing plan to build a strategy that will develop product appeal to identifiable market segments**. As the product develops in the mind of consumers, and as more competition enters the market, targeted segments become more and more finite. This is segmentation and niche marketing.

One of a marketing manager's responsibilities is determining if a product is a rising star, question mark, cash cow, or dog. In doing a review, determining consumer demand and where the product is located on the product demand life curve is without compromise. This Boston Consulting Group (BCG) product portfolio helps us understand these market conditions and the product demand life cycle explains the likely location of such a product prior to it being evaluated or assessed by the marketing manager.

By using these two marketing tools together or in conjunction with each other, the marketing manager knows where to look for these existing product types, how to assess their value and merit to the company and future earnings, and what to do with each of them.

STAR Product or Service
Market Conditions

- High market growth industry
  - Increasing consumer P/S demand.
  - Good P/S position in consumers mind
  - Competitors seek a market niche.

- High share of existing or current market
  - Consumers have yet to declare brand loyalty
  - Most current consumers prefer your P/S. (SWOT)

MKT215 and MKT 291 - James W. Stark

P. D. L. C. and a STAR P/S

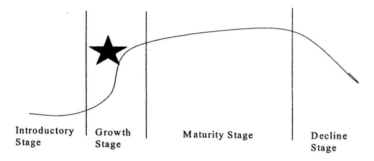

Introductory Stage | Growth Stage | Maturity Stage | Decline Stage

MKT215 and MKT 291 - James W. Stark

MARKETING STRATEGIES
for a STAR P/S!

- Create competitive barriers to entry.
- Assume the leadership role.
- Invest revenues earned from Cash Cow products into promoting STARS.
- Analyze Strengths and defend Weaknesses.

MKT215 and MKT 291 - James W. Stark

Student Notes:

97

QUESTION MARK Product or Service Market Conditions

- High growth industry
  - consumer awareness, comprehension and conviction is increasing.
  - competition is growing as new competitors enter the market.
- Low current market
  - consumers prefer a competing brand.

MKT215 and MKT 291 - James W. Stark

P. D. L. C. and the Question Mark P/S

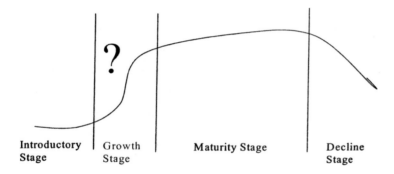

| Introductory Stage | Growth Stage | Maturity Stage | Decline Stage |

MKT215 and MKT 291 - James W. Stark

MARKETING STRATEGIES for a Question Mark P/S!

- Evaluate product positioning (SWOT)
- Consider Penetration Pricing
- Look for a Target Market Niche
  - TM=A^4+D)
- Consider dropping the P/S

MKT215 and MKT 291 - James W. Stark

Student Notes:

98

COW Product or Service
Market Conditions

- Low growth potential
  - Competition is stiff.
  - Mature market.
  - Differentiation is essential.
- High market share
  - Consumers prefer YOUR P/S over the competition.

MKT215 and MKT 291 - James W. Stark

P. D. L. C. and the Product Portfolio

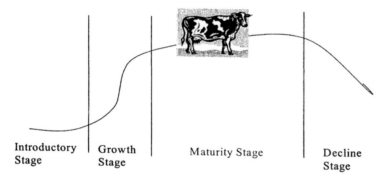

Introductory Stage | Growth Stage | Maturity Stage | Decline Stage

MKT215 and MKT 291 - James W. Stark

MARKETING STRATEGIES
for a COW P/S!

- Milk the product
  - Cash in on your strong market position.
  - Use revenues to support R&D or to promote Question Marks or STARS.
  - Try to maintain an industry leadership role and preserve cash flow.

MKT215 and MKT 291 - James W. Stark

Student Notes:

DOG Product or Service Market Conditions

– Low industry growth
  • Significant Competition.
  • Consumer demand is limited.
  • Substitutable P/S exist

– Low market share
  • consumers prefer COMPETITOR brands or demand is weak.

MKT215 and MKT 291 - James W. Stark

P. D. L. C. and a Dog P/S

Introductory Stage | Growth Stage | Maturity Stage | Decline Stage

MKT215 and MKT 291 - James W. Stark

MARKETING STRATEGIES for a DOG P/S!

• Sell P/S rights to a competitor.
• Drop the product (line).
• Invest in STARS & QUESTION MARKS.

MKT215 and MKT 291 - James W. Stark

Student Notes:

Consumer Behavior

Applying Marketing Tools and

Decision-making to Consumer Behavior

Although there are many areas of exciting discussion in the study of consumer behavior, some are outside of the purpose of this textbook. We are studying the tools of the profession that help us drive conclusions. There are such tools that are studied in Consumer Behavior. We will look at then integrate them into our marketing tool belt of previously studied tools.

The consumer adoption process has five primary levels. As consumers adapt to the use of products, they move the product through the PDLC. THIS IS WHAT CAUSES THE PDLC TO FUNCTION AS A MARKETING TOOL. It is driven by consumer demand and the study of consumer behavior identifies these groups or segments of consumers.

Once these five major segments of the consumers are identified, we will relate each to the PDLC. We will also relate it to the Bell Curve, once again proving that marketing tools work in concert with one another. If they don't then something is wrong with the product campaign, not the marketing tools.

Consumer P/S Adoption Segment

Innovators

– Those who will try any new product or service early on in the introduction stage of the PDLC.

Consumer P/S Adoption Segment

Adaptors

– Those who follow the lead of innovators. These consumers see the change is coming and are usually the consumer type responsible for getting the product demand cycle moving forward.

Consumer P/S Adoption Segment

Early Majority

– The new product or service is catching on. These consumer types push the P/S into a growth demand stage.

Notes:

Notes:
_____
_____
_____
_____
_____
_____
_____
_____
_____
_____
_____
_____
_____
_____
_____
_____
_____
_____
_____
_____
_____

Consumer P/S Adoption Segment

Late Majority

– Consumers who prefer a new product be field tested by other consumers prior to their making a purchase.

MKT312 – Consumer Behavior

Consumer P/S Adoption Segments

Laggards

Consumer type that prefers a good deal over being one of the first or second in a neighborhood to try a new P/S.

MKT312 – Consumer Behavior

Each of these consumer segments from innovators to laggards has a reason for trying a new product, but at different times along the adoption continuum or process. Unless there is an advertising campaign and a marketing manager that realizes these segments of consumers with similar mindsets exist, a product will never make it through the first year of product introduction.

What we need to know is what needs drive each of these segments to finally trying the new product. These needs must be recognized for what they are and be incorporated into the advertising campaign and the advertising pyramid.

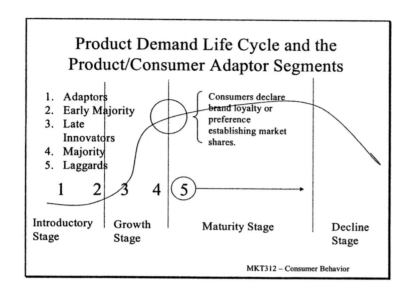

In this chart we see several things are going on at the same time. As different consumer segments PULL product into the growth stage (demand increases), a significant number of new identifiable consumer groups try the product for the first time.

The PULL is comes from increasing consumer demand for a product. The law of supply and demand that is practiced in a capitalistic economy makes product available. Where there are profits to be made, new businesses open.

Even after consumers begin to declare brand loyalties and preference there is that group of laggards. Statistically this is about 16% of the potential consumers of any given product. This group is not going to make a purchase decision until CONVINCED the product is well established, the bugs have been worked out, the price is right, and they are the only ones left on the block who don't own one. See the graph above. This also has much to do with the Advertising Pyramid and targeting market niches. Can you explain these connections?

What integrating the PDLC with the consumer adoption process tells us is that the majority of consumers who will purchase and try this product will have done so by the time the demand for the product reaches the maturity stage of the PDLC. This is when market share actually begins. The majority of potential consumers less the laggards have tried the product at least once by the time we reach this point on the PDLC called market share. This fact supports the principle that market share begins where the growth stage and the maturity stage cross.

The consumer adoption process has five basic steps to it. Every identifiable consumer group or segment must go through this process. Note how closely these steps parallel the Advertising Pyramid steps.

These adoption steps in no way suggest time continuums, rather a step-by-step process all consumers go through when evaluating or assessing a product or service for personal consumption. An Innovator is a consumer who may go through this process in a very short time period. The late majority takes longer, and in some instances, much longer to adopt the product for regular personal use.

Each group or adaptor segment goes through this five-step consumer adoption process: innovators, adaptors, early majority, late majority and laggards. This is true of every targeted consumer segment. Each will go through the Adoption Process steps. Even in our personal lives we do this. When we become aware of another individual we may share or may not share parts of our lives with them. If there is an interest we evaluate how much interest, test the waters of trust and confidence, then adopt the relationship for what we think it is or should be.

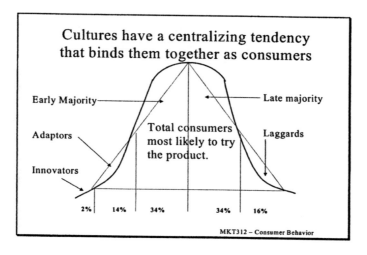

Cultures have a centralizing tendency
that binds them together as consumers

Early Majority — Late majority

Adaptors

Total consumers most likely to try the product.

Laggards

Innovators

2% | 14% | 34% | 34% | 16%

MKT312 – Consumer Behavior

"All cultures do not have a large middle class, but all cultures do tend to have a statistical centralizing tendency in all social and cultural areas of their lives."
- J. Stark

Most consumers will develop an awareness of a product, fewer will understand what the product is intended to do, and even fewer will take the time to determine if the claims of the product are realistic. Eighty-for percent of the total probable consumers of the product or service, in the above graph, will purchase and use the product or service before it reaches the maturity stage.

At the same time, 100% of a product or service's probable users do not respond at the same time and to the same advertising message. This resembles a learning curve. This in no way is to suggest that innovators and adaptors are the most faithful consumers. A combination of the first four product adoption segments, innovators, adaptors, early and late majority, will be the most faithful and dedicated user of the offered product or service.

As we move closer to the center of the Bell Curve and the Advertising Pyramid, we find the dedicated consumers of the product, those who are likely to be very brand loyal. Notice how the curve follows the consumer adoption process. That means, even in the maturity stage of the PDLC, laggards still exist and have yet to try or purchase the product for personal consumption. This also is why there can be SOME growth without stealing market share in the maturity stage of the product demand life cycle.

Good marketers realize that the Bell Curve is also statistically representative of every consumer segment. In these cases though, the centralizing tendency is the homogeneous problem being solved by purchasing and using the product. An example of this might be fast food restaurants. The spectrum of consumers who patronize these businesses ranges from the occasional to the dedicated fast food junky.

Another example of the above two marketing tools in action would be those who attend professional league sporting events. There is the fan that will attend an occasional game, those who get to a game as often as reasonable, and those who buy season tickets. The marketer's challenge is to identify this group, develop a primary message targeted to this group, than promote the message through a medium this group is most likely to read, see, watch, or hear.

Marketing principles closely parallel consumer problem recognition and problem processing or decision-making procedures. Consumers ask the same questions of themselves as marketing managers do of their products.

Marketing Principles	Consumer Decision Process
• Where are We Now?	• Problem Recognition • Information Search
• Where do We Wish to Be or Go?	• Alternative Evaluation • Purchase • Use/consumption
• What is our Best Option?	• Disposition • Evaluation

MKT312 – Consumer Behavior

Where are we now?

In a situation analysis, the marketing manager is first trying to determine what or if there is a consumer problem for which his product can be the preferred solution. He will try to determine if his product has a particular advantage or strength that the competition's product does not have and if the advantage can be exploited.

Where do we want to go?

Alternative evaluation, product purchase, and consumption expose the consumer and the marketing manager to their options and alternative courses of action. Consumers look for problems to be solved; marketers look for what groups or target markets accept their product as a solution to problems.

What is the best way to get there?

Disposition and evaluation to the consumer is after the fact. The consumer evaluates the products worth and problem solving capacity. The marketer measures the consumer's repeat purchase patterns and should come to the same conclusion, but after the fact.

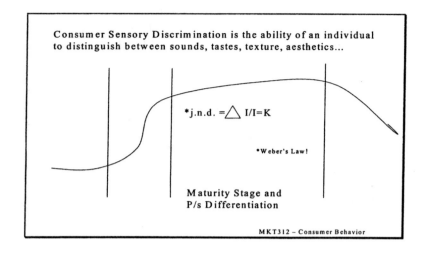

Consumer Sensory Discrimination is the ability of an individual to distinguish between sounds, tastes, texture, aesthetics...

$$*j.n.d. = \triangle I/I = K$$

*Weber's Law!

Maturity Stage and P/s Differentiation

MKT312 – Consumer Behavior

Just Noticeable Difference (j.n.d.) = the change in the P/S attribute divided by the initial attribute times the constant value given to our individual senses.

More practical than the formula itself is the knowledge that there is a threshold for every sense. When marketers are trying to distinguish between brands and competitors, these thresholds must be understood. This is particularly important in the late growth and early maturity stages of the PDLC. It becomes increasingly important, and to some degree, difficult to maintain sensory discrimination as the P/S enters the maturity stage of the PDLC. Attempts at product differentiation may or may not be noticeable by the consumer.

Marketers must ask, "What is that threshold of product differentiation as concerns the consumer perception?" A product that is differentiated by the manufacturer, but is not perceived as enough difference to warrant switching brands is wasted time and resources. The marketing goal is to find that consumer threshold of just noticeable difference (j.n.d). The advertising campaign can be built upon this difference. If not enough difference is perceived by the consumer to warrant switching brands, the advertising campaign is destined to failure.

How much difference is needed, per consumer perception and sensory discrimination, to cause a switch in product brands or choices? What is needed to move the product from the consumer's inert set to the elicited set of product considerations? We also need to know what it will take to move a product out of the rejection or inept set to neutral or acceptable grounds as a product of possible value to the consumer.

Perception of need requires consumers to assess both their desired state of being and their actual state of being. Within the desired state of being are two additional considerations that must be made by the consumer. First is the depth or amount of discrepancy between their actual and preferred or desired state of being. Second is the importance of the discrepancy.

Example: A great gap may exist between ones actual state of being and their preferred or desired state of being. But, the importance is not there for the consumer. This could be the difference between one's typing skills and the perceived importance of knowing how to type. This has also been a long time campaign icon of Buick advertisements. *"Wouldn't you really rather own a Buick"* so the question has been posed for years by Buick Corporation. Many consumers may answer this question yes, but owning a Buick is not as important as other demands on their lives.

On the other hand, a very small gap may exist between the desired and actual state of being, but the importance is significant to the consumer. A college student may not need a new pair of shoes or clothes, but the pending occasion makes that need very important. The difference between a "B-" and a "B" is statistically insignificant regarding student performance in the subject, but the importance of the "B" may be very significant or important to the student.

It is critical to understand consumer behavior has one consistent or centralizing tendency. That is, to solve problems in their lives. Any product or service purchased by consumers has the sole purpose of solving a consumer problem perception.

The challenge is to understand the factors that drive consumer behavior and how to position a product or service as the best available solution to the consumer's problem.

Consumer Behavior - James W. Stark

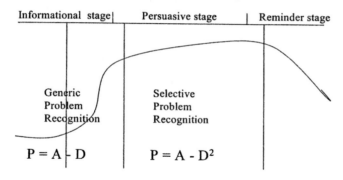

Activating Consumer Problem Recognition/PDLC

Informational stage | Persuasive stage | Reminder stage

Generic Problem Recognition

Selective Problem Recognition

$P = A - D$

$P = A - D^2$

Consumer Behavior - James W. Stark

If the marketing manager is proactive, s/he may wish to "activate" the consumer perception of his or her need (problem). Problem recognition by consumers is of low importance due to a lack of *awareness, understanding, or conviction (*Advertising Pyramid) that a problem exists.

The need for information is critical. **Generic problem** recognition is usually an industry wide effort and happens early in the PDLC. Consumers do not have an operational grasp of the product functions or its capacities. The competition is still somewhat limited, but is beginning to develop. The advertising message will be more **generic** than brand specific. **The goal is to activate initial problem recognition** in the minds of the adaptors and early majority consumers. This is early in the PDLC $(P = D - A)$

Selective problem recognition in consumers comes when differentiation of products is essential due to the competitive nature of the market. We move from Target Markets to Target Niches. Problem recognition centers on market niches. Efforts are made to stimulate unique consumer problem solutions. This takes us back to the $P=D^2-A$ word formula. Marketers must try to influence the magnitude of the consumer's perception of the discrepancy, the importance of the discrepancy, or both (D^2)

```
┌─────────────────────────────────────────────────┐
│                                                 │
│        Consumer Categorization of Products      │
│                                                 │
│                                                 │
│      Evoked          Inert          Inept       │
│      ‾‾‾‾‾‾          ‾‾‾‾‾          ‾‾‾‾‾        │
│                       ▲                         │
│                                                 │
│      Consumers intentionally or inadvertently assign │
│      products and services to one of these three     │
│      categories.                                │
│                                                 │
└─────────────────────────────────────────────────┘
```

```
┌─────────────────────────────────────────────────┐
│                                                 │
│        Developing Consumer Preference           │
│          Or Noticeable Differences              │
│    Consumers divide products into three perception or preference │
│    sets: evoked, inert, and inept.              │
│                                                 │
│    ┌───────────────────────────────────────┐   │
│    │ Evoked sets are product options that come to a consumer's │
│    │ mind when a personal need is identified by the consumer.   │
│    │ Inert sets are those products that do not come to mind during │
│    │ the consumer search.                  │   │
│    │ Inept sets are those products that come to mind, but not as │
│    │ viable choices to the consumer.       │   │
│    └───────────────────────────────────────┘   │
│                                                 │
└─────────────────────────────────────────────────┘
```

The marketing issue here is moving one's product into a consumer's EVOKED SET and then working on making it the product of choice or preference. This is the essence of this book. Consider what tools of the trade have been studied that will attract, detract, or make a product fit, by choice or default, into any of these three sets.

Everything we have studied boils down to this consumer consideration. Is the product or service a viable solution to an identified consumer problem? Are there products that have never made it to the evoked set and languish in the shadows of "not being recognized" as a value or solution to a problem? Maybe not even known to exist as a product?

Worse case scenario…is your product one that has been condemned by consumers to the prison walls of ineptness, not capable of solving a problem, poor value for dollars spent, beyond ones' reach? Use these tools to analyze, assess, and then build strategy, strategy that will work. Guessing is no longer a viable option in a world economy where the other competitors KNOW THE TOOLS OF THE PROFESSION!

Building Product Categories

And Pricing Strategies

We can't leave the study of marketing tools without addressing all of the marketing mix. One of these 4 Ps is price. Too often marketing textbooks get pricing strategy confused with pricing tactics.

Strategy is the umbrella under which tactics are developed. Tactics are the day-to-day activities and strategy is the guiding light. An example of this might be in distribution. There are three types of distribution (placement according to the marketing mix and the 4 Ps):

1.   Intensive
2.   Selective
3.   Exclusive

Each of these is a distribution strategy. Where the products get delivered to is the tactic. An intensive strategy does not tell the marketing manager where to place product, only that it is to be readily available for consumers to purchase.

A selective strategy is a little tougher on the tactical people in marketing. This strategy states that the product will be a shopping item. It must only be available at limited outlets and retailers. Deciding through which retailers to distribute product is the tactic.

Exclusive distribution strategy is even tougher for tactical planners. The placement of products will be exclusive to territories and dealers. The tactical team has to figure out where and who will be the product retailer. This can become a tactical nightmare.

The same is true about pricing strategy. Too often a student learns that **30-day/net 10** is a strategy. Not true! This is a tactic. The same is true about any pricing methodology that gives instructions on how it is to be done and the numbers with which the marketing manager must work. This includes FOB, cost PLUS pricing, standard percentage markups, stated discount percentages, odd or psychological pricing. These are tactics, not strategies.

Let's look a several major pricing strategies, than conclude by determining where in the PDLC each would be most effective.

Pricing Strategies

Promotional Pricing:

This type of pricing is defined by its start date, stop date tactic. The price is a temporary discount that will return to full price after the promotion. The beginning date and the ending date of the "promotion" is published. PDLC hint: It should be obvious that if something is promotionally priced, PRICE must be a consumer issue.

Penetration Pricing:

This strategy has two specific and different uses. The purpose of the first strategy is to capture as much market as possible, keeping the price low long enough that it discourages competitors from entering the market. Competitors only jump in where profits are to be made. If banks rates are higher, then a CD makes more sense and a lot less hassle. When is this strategy best used?

PDLC hint: This strategy is designed to keep other competitors from entering the market.

The second way to use a penetration pricing strategy is to enter an existing market with a low price in order to attract or steal market share. Then, raise prices at a later date to the levels of most of your competitors (see competitive pricing).

PDLC hint: …to attract or steal market share!

Competitive Pricing:

Competitive pricing means pricing is NOT THE ISSUE. When all items are priced within a small range of each other, this is competitive pricing in practice. This is often done in candy vending machines. Every candy bar in it is $1.00. Gasoline pricing is another example of this strategy in use. Competitive wages mean similar to the wages being paid in the rest of the industry. It doesn't mean higher wages.

PDLC hint: Existing products like candy, gasoline, etc are priced using this strategy.

Comparison Pricing:

Our price/Their price is seen on the same sticker. How much that difference will be is the tactic. Sometimes retailers will re-price an item with a store sticker, but deliberately not cover the MSRP (manufacturers suggested retail price) that is on the package.

PDLC hint: The purpose is for the consumer to SEE the two prices side-by-side.

Prestige Pricing:

This is a deliberate high price on an item. It is assumed by the marketing people that image is what is being sought after by the consumer. Image has a price tag as it creates exclusivity in product ownership.

PDLC hint: If something is vogue or more prestigious than something else, we have more than one product in the market, right?

Skimming Pricing:

When there is little competition, a provider of a product or service that is in high demand can "skim" off extra cream from the high price on the product. Every time the gasoline conglomerates scream "shortage," the price at the pump skyrockets even if the price at the crude oil level didn't really go up that much. This is a skimming strategy.

PDLC hint: If there is no direct or substitutable competitor for a product that has a significant consumer demand, there must be no competition.

Note that these pricing strategies are a guiding light to the retailer or marketing manager. The numbers they put into these strategies is the tactic. It is critical to the successful marketing or sales manager to know which pricing strategy is the best fit in their market mix.

Can you assign each strategy to a most likely to work tactical location on the below Product Demand Life Cycle? Locate the earliest time of the consumer demand life cycle when these pricing strategies may be most effective.

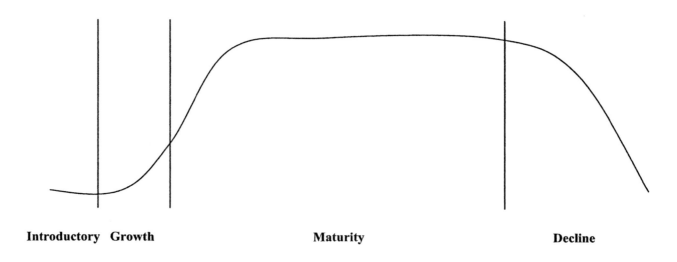

Introductory Growth   Maturity   Decline

Credits and Reading Sources:

Marketing Curriculum Committee:
    James W. Stark, MM; Department Chair (Muskegon Campus)
    Robert Payne, Vice-President and Dean of Business (Port Huron Campus)
    Sue Cathcart, MBA; Dean of Business (Auburn Hills Campus)
    Joe Pepoy, MBA; Dean of Business (Mount Clemens Campus)
    Harold Krul, MBA (marketing instructor)

Focus Group:

Patricia Bectel	(Quality Stores)
Chris Guerrero	(Mail Box, ETC)
Amanda Jenson	(Orchard View Travel Agency)
Nathen Kooi	(College student)
Stephen Lindgren	(Lamar Inc.)
Patricia Redeker	(Maggie's Baskets)
Jennifer Way	(College student)

David W. Stewart, "From Methods and Projects to Systems and Process: The Evolution of Marketing Research Techniques," *Marketing Research.*

"Why Some Customers are More Equal Than Others, *Fortune* (September 19, 1994)

Carl McDaniel and Roger Gates, *"Contemporary Marketing,"* Fourth Edition, South-Western Publishing

Ronald B. Marks, *"Personal Selling: A Relationship Approach,"* Sixth Edition, Prentice Hall Publishing

John Naisbitt, *"Megatrands: Ten New Directions Transforming Our Lives,"* Warner Books

Donald W. Jungenheimer and Gordon White, *"Basic Advertising,"* South-Western Publishing

Charles L. Martin, *"Your New Business, A personal Plan for Success,"* Crisp Publications

William G. Zikmund and Michael d'Amico, *"Marketing,"* Fifth Edition, West Publishing

J. Paul Peter and James H. Donnelly, Jr., *"A Preface to Marketing Management,"* 6th Edition, Irwin Publishing

Stuart Crainer, *"The Ultimate Business Library,"* American Management Association, Capstone Publishing Limited

Secondary Sources – Selected Periodicals and Trade Publications from which market analysis subject matter is available and have assisted this author in his study of marketing, analysis, integrated and process thinking.

Advertising Age
American Demographics
American Economist
Business Economics
Business Marketing
Business Week
Convenience Store Merchandising
Chain Store Age
Direct Marketing
Forbes
Fortune
Harvard Business Review
Hardware Age
Lawn & Garden Marketing
Michigan Newspaper Publishers Association
National Rifleman's Association
Retailing
Sales & Marketing Management
Supermarket News
United States Census Report

Although no information was taken directly from any of these publications, the reading of these publications has aided this author to better understand the business of marketing and the consumer. Add to this 29 years of working in corporate America, 12 years of college level teaching in marketing, plus owning and operating a construction company, the result is this study guide; a process of thinking through and developing a use for marketing tools as a checks and balance in market decision-making.

Author: James W. Stark, MM.
            Marketing Department Chair
            Baker College – Muskegon Campus